creative spaces
for kids

Lauren Floodgate

Nikki Haslam

Gill Brewis

Karen O'Grady

hamlyn

First published in Great Britain in 2002
by Hamlyn, a division of
Octopus Publishing Group Ltd
2–4 Heron Quays, London E14 4JP

First published in paperback in 2003

ISBN 0 600 61003 9

A CIP catalogue record for this book is available
from the British Library

Printed and bound in China

10 9 8 7 6 5 4 3 2 1

In describing all the projects in this book, every care
has been taken to recommend the safest methods
of working. Before starting any task, you should be
confident that you know what you are doing, and
that you know how to use all tools and equipment
safely. The publishers cannot accept any legal
responsibility or liability for accidents or damage
arising from the use of any items mentioned, or in
the carrying out of any of the projects described.

creative spaces for kids

contents

How to use this book

The book includes 16 room designs ranging from a nursery to a teenage den. Each room design includes both practical and inspirational ideas, from imaginative colour schemes to novel storage. Step-by-step projects, colour swatches and finishing touches all guide you to achieving the look you want, so you can recreate a room in its entirety, or just take elements that appeal to you and adapt them to a design of your own.

Icons

For explanation, see panel (right).

Colour swatches

Each room design is also accompanied by a colour swatch. The dominant colours have been picked out so that you can see at a glance the colour scheme and how many different paints each room would need.

Step-by-step instructions

Each project is explained in easy-to-follow stages. Use the list of tools and materials to check that you have got together everything you need before you start work.

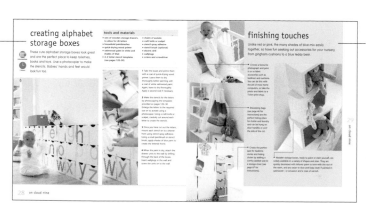

Finishing touches

Each design finishes with some extra ideas that could be added to the room to give it that individual touch.

Icons

Each room design is accompanied by icons that identify certain features or characteristics of the design.

projects especially for boys

projects especially for girls

storage solutions

projects on a budget

study area

room to grow – a room that can grow with your child without too much transformation

helping hand – projects that your child can help with

entertaining area

play area

easy

intermediate

advanced

30 minutes

1 hour

2 hours

3 hours

4 hours

5 hours

6 hours

depends on size of room

Project times:
Please note that the timing of all projects excludes paint drying time.

Steps for planning and decorating a child's room

1 Get the basics right. Decide what you want the room to do and make a list.

2 Decide on a budget and style, then collect together samples, swatches and paint cards. Make a mood board. This is simply a large board on to which you stick pictures, photographs, fabric swatches and paint cards, all of which, when put together, will provide you with a feel for the finished room. Assembling a mood board will help crystallize your ideas.

3 Draw a plan of the room and decide where everything will live. Check that you have the space for any large new items of furniture and that you have sufficient storage.

4 Have a sort out and decide what is staying, going or being 'made over'.

5 Plan your decorating. Will you be bedroomless while the work is in progress?

6 Clear the room as far as possible and give yourself plenty of space to work in. Protect floors with dust sheets.

7 Prepare your surfaces thoroughly. Time spent now will be time saved later. Buy tester pots, paint squares on the wall and decide on the colour only when the paint is dry.

8 Assemble your materials – write a checklist and don't start work until everything is to hand.

9 Follow a logical order of work – start with the woodwork, then ceiling, walls and finally floors.

Creative techniques (above) Once you have mastered how to stencil, stamp or sew, a whole new world of creative decoration opens up.

Self-assembly (left) Ready-to-assemble furniture can be a huge money-saver if you are decorating on a tight budget. Treat a basic shape as a starting point to customize as you want.

Working with wood (below) Adaptable tools and materials such as MDF make constructing simple pieces in wood a whole lot easier.

Furniture and storage

Although child-sized furniture looks cute it is not alwa[y]
practical, so choose your furniture wisely. If the room i[s]
to be used for feeding, it needs to include a comfortab[le]
Make sure you try before you buy. For many mothers f[eeding]
takes prolonged periods so check you have somewhere [to rest]
your arms to prevent you from having to support the e[ntire]
weight of the baby during feeding.

You may also wish to include a changing area. Thi[s may]
be either a changing mat laid on the floor when requir[ed, or]
a changing unit, a little like a small cupboard with add[ed]
height on the top three edges to stop the baby rolling [off]
and a padded surface (see page 38). This saves lifting t[he baby]
up and down but takes up valuable space in a small ro[om.]

Babies come with stuff – loads of it – so ensure you [have]
adequate storage space in the form of shelves, cupboa[rds,]
drawers, peg rails or wheeled containers. Items for disp[lay]
can be hung from peg rails or the top of wardrobes, le[ss]
attractive essentials such as nappies can be discreetly hi[dden]
away from view. Varnished or wipeable materials will be [easy]
to keep clean. This may be an opportunity to give a ne[w lease]
of life to an old cupboard or chest of drawers. Somethi[ng]
friends or family would be glad to be rid of, or a bargai[n from]
a local house clearance auction can be transformed wit[h a lick]
of paint and perhaps new knobs.

The cot is an essential piece of furniture. You may b[e lucky]
enough to borrow one that can be cleaned up with a w[ipe,]
a coat of fresh paint and the addition of a new mattress[. If you]
do need to buy one, buy wisely. Many now double as a [junior]
bed and have easy-to-remove sides, saving you the add[ition]
of a new bed in two years' time.

Very young children generally have few clothes that [may]
require hanging, so a chest of drawers may suffice with [the]
addition of a peg rail for the odd item that needs hangi[ng.]
You will need lots of high-level storage for baby and en[ough]
adult-orientated storage to make taking care of baby ea[sy.]

Colours and materials

A little understanding of how colours work together will simplify the process of putting together a colour scheme. All colours are derived from the three primary colours: red, yellow and blue. Mixing primary colours makes secondary colours; red and blue makes purple, for example. All other colours are called tertiary colours and are made from a combination of primary and secondary colours. Tones are produced by lightening or darkening colours with the addition of white or black.

To use the colour wheel pick a colour; the colours on either side of your chosen colour will tone with it, the colour directly opposite will complement and contrast with it. For a harmonizing feel choose colours of the same intensity; the greater the difference in intensity the more a colour will stand out. Chimney breasts or window walls look effective when highlighted in this way. To bring a high ceiling down paint it the same colour as the walls, to give a room height paint the ceiling a lighter shade than the walls.

Colours have definite warming or cooling properties. A room that is very cold can be warmed up with rich colours; a small room can be made to look larger if painted with light tones of the same colour. If you are unsure of your decorating abilities use light, pastel shades since they are easy to mix and match. Dark colours are useful for covering blemishes and camouflaging unevenness. They will also conceal dirt and cope better with general wear and tear.

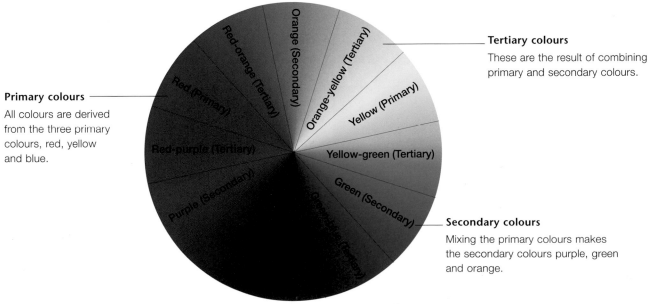

Tertiary colours
These are the result of combining primary and secondary colours.

Primary colours
All colours are derived from the three primary colours, red, yellow and blue.

Secondary colours
Mixing the primary colours makes the secondary colours purple, green and orange.

Baby's bed (right)
Choose between a
traditional cot or one
that converts into a bed
for a toddler.

Soft furnishings
(below) Pretty bedding
and cushion covers are
easy to make, but do
check that the materials
you use are suitable
for a baby.

Flooring (above) Choose easy-to-clean surfaces that are warm and
not too hard on bare feet.

Comfort (right)
When furnishing a
nursery, don't forget to
include somewhere soft
and cushioned where
you can sit and nurse
or comfort your baby.

Lighting (above) A table lamp will provide a soft glow that will give you enough
light to see by without waking the baby.

Flooring

Nursery flooring needs to be practical, hardwearing, washable
and warm. Floorboards may look good but they are hard
underfoot, often uneven and can be draughty and hard to
keep clean. Laminate flooring or washable carpet is the best
choice. Laminate provides a smooth surface that can be swept
and washed easily. It is warm underfoot, easy to lay and
relatively inexpensive. Carpet can be laid in one piece or as
carpet tiles. Either is warm underfoot, easy to lay and relatively
inexpensive. Carpet offers many of the same benefits as
laminate and many types now come treated with a stain
repellent, some are even bleach scrubbable. If your child is an
asthmatic you will need to pick your flooring carefully.

Lighting

Lighting is the most overlooked aspect of decorating but it is
one that can make a vast difference to the finished effect. You
will need dual-purpose lighting in a nursery – bright overhead
light for dressing and play, warm low-level light for feeding
and bedtime. Decorative bedside lamps come in all manner
of shapes and styles and the range available is vast.

Walls

You will be spoilt for choice now that there are so many lovely
wallpapers and borders around and the ranges of paint colours
are growing by the day. Many companies supply coordinating
wallpapers, borders and curtains. If, however, this look is a
little over the top for your taste, why not mix and match
papers and paint? You could have one papered wall with three
complementary painted walls or painted walls with a frieze or
border of stamps or stencils. So that your freshly decorated
room remains looking freshly decorated, try and use wipeable
papers and washable paints, avoiding flat matt emulsion and
solid coloured wallpapers. Be prepared for accidents, spills and
tears and keep a little paint and wallpaper for touching up later.

Painting Tester pots are a real boon to decorators. Use them to achieve a special effect (left) as well as trying out different shades in situ (right).

Bags of space (below) Drawstring bags are easy to run up and have a multitude of uses: small ones can be home to tiny toys, larger ones make great laundry bags.

Finishing touches

★ Print your baby's hands and feet for decorative purposes, using embossing inks and powder

★ Buy a handle-making kit, take casts of your baby's hands and use them to make individual handles for furniture

★ Make a name plaque

★ Paint delicate stars and moons on the ceiling using glow-in-the-dark paints, which will come alive when the lights are off

Checklist

• blackout curtains or blinds

• machine-washable bedlinen

• comfy chair for breastfeeding

• baby changing area

• drawer and cupboard storage for baby accessories and clothes

• coat hooks or peg rails

• cot or cot-bed

• varnished or wipeable surfaces

• hardwearing, warm flooring

• dual-purpose lighting

• bright, durable paintwork and wallpaper

Toddlers and young children

Many of the points to bear in mind when decorating a baby's room still hold fast with a toddler or young child's room. The use of the bedroom is now changing, however, and for many children the bedroom doubles as a playroom. It may also be a room that has to be shared with a sibling. Young children are little people who are more than capable of telling you their likes and dislikes, which makes it fun to decorate for them! This is the age group with which you can probably be most adventurous. This should be a room just for them, a room in which they want to play and where they feel happy going to sleep – a room in fact that should be so enticing they will want to go to bed!

The rules for surfaces and finishes are similar to those for a nursery, but this time round think robust.

Textiles

Blinds and curtains should still obscure as much light as possible, especially important in the summer with light mornings and evenings. Machine-washable fabrics are desirable, as well as those that are crease resistant and suitable for tumble drying. Think 'washable, wipeable, cleanable' when buying anything for a young child's bedroom.

Furniture

It is now time to replace the cot. Starter beds are scaled-down versions of single beds. They are low to the floor and you will need bedlinen to fit. A full-size single can be used into tweenage, takes standard linen and provides useful storage space beneath. Bunk beds are the ideal solution if space is short or siblings have

Toyland (above and right) For those times when it seems as if dolls and furry animals have completely taken over your child's room, plan a 'home' into which they can be tidied. It could be a large chest the child has helped decorate or a cupboard painted like a house, with shelves to accommodate the inhabitants.

to share a room. Children sharing rooms may be able to share a set of bunkbeds but they will still need privacy – freestanding shelf units or room dividers or partitions between single beds can be used to provide this. Study beds incorporate study areas and additional seating beneath a bunk bed but these are really suitable only for children of five years and upwards. The choice of bed ultimately depends on space, budget and end use. If storage is short a divan will give you useful 'hidden' storage space for clothes, shoes or toys. And even the plainest bed will have scope for decoration. Paint or colourwash pine, cover a headboard in bold fabric or cut a new, shaped headboard from MDF and paint it as you wish. For a pretty princess bedroom try adding a simple mosquito net or a swathe of netting fabric above the bed to form a decorative canopy.

Storage

Your children will soon be acquiring more and more possessions, all of which need a home. Some can be hidden away in wardrobes and cupboards, toy chests and chests of drawers, some they will want to display. Consider a cover for a radiator to protect small fingers; it will also provide a useful storage shelf. Attach hooks to the back of doors and hang up clothes and toys in fabric bags. A net hammock can be hung up and filled with toys, as can pocketed, fabric storage tidies.

By providing low-level storage a toddler can be encouraged to put away toys. Safety is paramount; don't store things away at high level as this might encourage a climb and then a fall. Look for furniture that incorporates slam-proof hinges.

Flooring

Flooring surfaces should be easy to clean and resistant to spills; laminate is ideal for children of this age. It is available in many wood finishes and colours, is easy to lay and provides a clean and safe surface to play on. If you are considering carpet, choose a stain-resistant one; a patterned or textured carpet will also be more forgiving. Solid-coloured, smooth pile carpet will require endless vacuuming.

A room with a theme
Planning a themed room can be great fun. Coordinated bedding can be a starting point (above) or you may prefer to keep to plain bedlinen (left) that will still be usable when the theme has outworn its interest.

Storage (below)
When children have to share a room, make sure they each have somewhere to store their own treasures.

Low-level storage
(right and below)
Chests of drawers
and tall cupboards are
often less user-friendly
than open-topped
boxes that can be slid
out of sight under
the bed.

Decorating projects
(right) Throughout the
book there are ideas
to which children
themselves can
contribute, such
as dressing up
lampshades to
complement a
room scheme.

Lighting

Lighting should be bright and overhead allowing for safe play. For children who don't like to sleep in the dark there is the option of plug-in low-level lighting. Table lights are very versatile and there are some wonderfully imaginative designs around, but make sure that there are not any cables left trailing, and use safety covers on plug sockets that are not in use.

Walls

New paint formulations mean we now have access to bedroom-friendly fragranced emulsions allowing a room to be redecorated and slept in immediately. Many emulsions are now wipeable and scrub resistant, essential especially for the lower level area of wall, which may be regularly bashed and bumped. Most satinwood paints provide a wipeable finish that is chip resistant to everyday wear and tear. These can also be applied without a base coat and come in quick-drying, low-odour finishes. Blackboard paints, both the sprayable and paint-brushable versions, allow a wall or door to be transformed into a blackboard (see page 68). Glow-in-the-dark, glitter, fluorescent and textured paints provide scope for even the most ambitious of projects.

If you prefer wallpaper, the choice is as broad as it is for paint. Choose from paste-free horizontal stripes, jumbo borders, friezes, moveable motifs, wipeable, washable and easily removable papers. There are also decorating aids like stamps and stencils.

Murals are perfect for this age range and you don't need to be Van Gogh to paint one (see pages 44 and 59). They are an inexpensive way to transform a room and a great way of using up leftover paint or tester pots. Paint is a wonderful medium for decorating – a band of yellow and a band of blue and you have a beach; wiggly bands of blue and you are under the sea. With a mural you are limited only by your children's imaginations. And what is best about murals is that the kids can help you paint them. Let them add a fish or a hand-print, a name or a flower or give them a brush and let them paint in the eyes. Don't worry if the finish isn't 100 per cent – it's their room and they will love it!

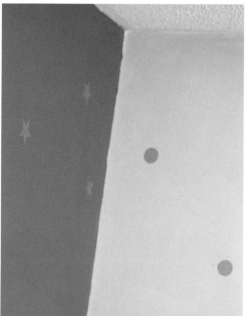

Blackboard (above)
Not all classrooms
have blackboards any
more, but drawing on
your own wall holds
great appeal for
young children.

Sweet sleep (above
right) This is a bed that
will hold its appeal right
through to adulthood.

Wall painting (left)
You don't have to be an
artist to add interest to
a wall: stamped stars
or sponged blobs will
brighten up any
plain wall.

Finishing touches

★ *Stamp, paint or dye the bedlinen*

★ *Decorate plain shelves with a fancy moulding or MDF trim*

★ *Makeover an old wardrobe or chest*

★ *Paint a height chart on the wall (see page 27)*

Checklist

• *blackout curtains or blinds*

• *easily washable bedlinen*

• *starter bed/single bed/bunk beds*

• *low-level storage for toys and books*

• *hanging storage for clothes*

• *furniture with slam-proof hinges*

• *easy-to-clean flooring*

• *bright lighting and nightlight*

• *wipeable paintwork and wallpaper*

• *imaginative, bold room theme*

Tweenagers & teenagers

The decorating rules change yet ágain – you are now decorating for a young adult who will have very strong opinions of their own. Tweenagers and teenagers don't want to be reminded of childhood; they want a more adult look. Think one-room living rather than bedroom. The bedroom now becomes truly multi-functional. It is a room in which to sleep, study and relax, and it needs to be decorated so as to deliver on all three levels. You may have to draw the line at some suggestions but try and go along with them. Giving your children a room of their very own is a shrewd move – they will enjoy spending time in this room, and their belongings can be confined to one place, freeing up other areas of the house.

Textiles
At this age the kids will want to help so why not let them tie-dye their own bedlinen or customize a blind (see pages 88, 110 and 117)? A border of ribbon or braid or a band of contrasting coloured fabric may be all it takes to transform an inexpensive pair of curtains. Lampshades and lamps can be 'made over' in much the same way (see pages 75, 86 and 106).

Furniture and storage
There is plenty of multi-functional furniture to choose from, including study bunks incorporating beds, desks and sofa seating – the ideal solution if space is tight. Some also incorporate a futon-style extra chair that can be extended to provide an additional bed. The seating area provides an area in which to relax, somewhere where they can watch TV

A space of your own
(above) For a teenager a place to call your own is very important. Try to go along with their ideas about what they would like, within reason.

Delicate designs
(right) Not all young people want off-the-wall designs or loud colours. This teenager's room gave her just the touch of sophistication she wanted.

or surf the Internet. This style of bed is reasonably inexpensive and universally available. For a room with more space a divan might be the better option if storage space is required. The drawers are easily accessible and are ideal for clothing. You may even want to consider a second bed for when their friends stay over.

Older children, especially girls, have more clothes, so a wardrobe is essential. Choose from freestanding, built-in or modular furniture.

A desk and suitable chair are essential and you may need space for a computer and printer. Wall-mounted monitors free up valuable desk space and many computer desks include drawers for stowing away keyboards when not in use. Shelving and storage will need consideration. Books, sports kit and all other paraphernalia will need a home. Give them somewhere to store magazines and CDs and their rooms will stay tidier. An ottoman, wheeled plastic boxes, laundry basket, hanging storage and extra shelves will all help. With homework being so important, how about making a notice board or pinboard (see pages 71, 93 and 111)? Gluing cork tiles above a desk is an inexpensive and quick alternative – just use small map pins to pin up bits and pieces.

Lighting

Lighting should allow the child to work, relax and play in their room. Overhead lighting is essential, as is a directional desk lamp and a bedside lamp.

Walls

Older children still love bold colours but many will be refining their tastes and you may find they prefer a subtler scheme. Paint effects can be used to great effect if a soft colourwash, stone-washed denim or glitter glaze is required. Themed wallpaper and borders of the latest band or group may also be popular. Children's tastes change quickly, however, so decorate inexpensively as you may be redecorating within two or three years.

Finishing touches

★ *Make beanbags or a heap of scatter cushions for the bed or floor (see pages 105 and 116)*
★ *Mount a mirror on the back of a door*
★ *A dressing table area will be welcomed by most girls*
★ *Let them put up posters – there are many fixatives available that won't damage the walls*

Checklist

- *multi-functional furniture*
- *additional seating (beanbags, floor cushions, sofa) for friends*
- *desk and chair*
- *computer, TV, music system*
- *additional space for clothes*
- *shelving and storage for books, sports kit, magazines and CDs*
- *laundry basket*
- *notice board or pinboard*
- *lighting – overhead, desk and bedside*
- *bold colours or subtle paint effects*

Children develop so fast it is hard to believe that yesterday's babe-in-arms will be tomorrow's teenager. As they grow, their room will reflect their changing tastes and requirements, from the reassuring cosiness of the nursery to the semi-independence of a teenager's retreat. The 16 rooms featured here graduate through all the stages, and contain many ideas that can be adapted as your child grows up.

from nursery to teenage den

on cloud nine

Oozing with style, this cool, calm nursery is practical, too. There is room for mum to relax plus quirky ideas to help baby to learn and play. For a space that feels light and bright, opt for lots of brilliant white, splashes of blue and a theme of clouds. Storage is definitely required when it comes to a nursery, as a baby comes with loads of toys, clothes, accessories and general clutter.

projects

- toy-box train

- child's height chart

- alphabet storage boxes

finishing touches

- photograph printing

- drawstring bags

- padded seat

- wooden storage boxes

practical elements

Light, bright colours give a fresh and airy feel •

Mother, as well as baby, will need to rest in the nursery, so a • storage box doubles as a comfortable padded seat

The scheme incorporates a host of handy storage tricks •

Tools for learning and playing are combined •

1   2   3

making a toy-box train

For a great storage solution that is also loads of fun, paint pine storage boxes in shades of blue then add castors and link the boxes with rope to create a play train. Guaranteed to make clearing up lots of fun!

tools and materials

- 2 or more wooden storage boxes with handles
- household paintbrushes
- quick-drying wood primer
- satinwood paint in blue
- screws and screwdriver
- 4 castors per box
- length of rope or thick cord
- sharp knife (such as a Stanley knife) for trimming the rope

1 Prime the boxes with a coat of quick-drying wood primer. Leave them to dry before painting with a coat of satinwood paint then leave them to dry once more.

2 Turn each box upside down and screw a castor to each corner.

3 Link the boxes together by threading a length of rope or cord through the box handles. Tie a large knot at each end of the rope to secure and trim away any excess.

painting a height chart

easy

2 hours

Paint a useful and fun height chart in a child's bedroom and add a splash of bright colour at the same time. Just mark on the heights in chalk. Don't forget to include the date as well.

tools and materials

- pencil
- steel tape measure
- long rule
- spirit level
- low-tack masking tape
- emulsion paint in 5 different shades of blue
- household paintbrushes
- permanent marker pen

1 Mark a pencil mark on the wall immediately above the skirting board. Measure 135cm (53in) up the wall and mark a second point. Join the points with a pencil line, using the spirit level to check it is exactly vertical.

2 Measure 40cm (16in) to the right or left of the first point and repeat the process, then join up the top points, again checking with the spirit level that the line is horizontal.

3 Using the low-tack masking tape, outline the rectangle on the wall, keeping the tape on the outside of the pencil lines. The tape at the bottom of the rectangle should be on the skirting board itself.

4 Divide the depth of the rectangle by five then apply lengths of the masking tape across the rectangle to mask horizontal lines at each of the divisions.

5 Using five shades of the same colour, start painting in the rectangles, starting at the bottom with the darkest shade of paint.

6 When the paint is dry, carefully remove the masking tape. Using a marker pen and rule, draw a thin vertical line up one edge of the rectangle. You can mark the height changes directly on to the wall as your child grows.

creating alphabet storage boxes

intermediate

3 hours

These cute alphabet storage boxes look great and are the perfect place to keep toiletries, books and toys. Use a photocopier to make the stencils. Babies' hands and feet would look fun too.

tools and materials

- sets of wooden storage drawers, to allow for 26 letters
- household paintbrushes
- quick-drying wood primer
- satinwood paint in white and shades of blue
- A–Z letter stencil templates (see pages 122–30)
- sheets of acetate
- craft knife or scalpel
- stencil spray adhesive
- stencil brush (optional)
- electric drill
- wallplugs
- screws and screwdriver

1 Take the boxes and prime them with a coat of quick-drying wood primer. Leave them to dry thoroughly before painting with a coat of white satinwood paint. Again, leave to dry thoroughly. Apply a second coat if necessary.

2 Make the stencils for the letters by photocopying the templates provided on pages 122–30. Enlarge the letters to the required size on to acetate using a photocopier. Using a craft knife or scalpel, carefully cut around each letter to create the stencils.

3 Once you have cut out the letters, mount each stencil on to a drawer front using stencil spray adhesive. Using a small paintbrush or stencil brush, apply shades of blue paint to create the lettered fronts.

4 When the paint is dry, attach the drawer units to the wall by drilling through the back of the boxes. Insert wallplugs in the wall and screw the units on to the wall.

finishing touches

Unlike red or pink, the many shades of blue mix easily together, so have fun seeking out accessories for your nursery, from gingham cushions to a blue teddy bear.

• Choose a favourite photograph and print it on to fabric accessories such as bedlinen and cushions. You can do this with the aid of most home computers, or take the photo and fabric to a T-shirt print shop.

• Drawstring bags (see page 46 for instructions) are the perfect hiding place for clutter and laundry and can be hung on door handles.

• Create the perfect spot for bedtime stories and hiding clutter by adding a comfy padded seat to a storage chest (see page 67 for instructions).

• Wooden storage boxes, ready to paint or stain yourself, are widely available in a variety of shapes and sizes. They are quickly decorated with leftover paint to tone with the rest of the room, and are easier to dust and keep clean if painted in satinwood – or emulsion and a coat of varnish.

duck nursery

A bright, stimulating environment in which to spend time and play is essential for a new baby. A simple motif is all it takes to develop a theme. Small children love animal motifs, so brightly coloured ducks in different guises are an ideal choice.

projects

• stencilled lampshades

• decorative border of stencilled ducks

• hand-painted duck plaque

finishing touches

• stencilled uplighter

• colour-coordinated storage boxes

• carpet tiles

• handy storage unit

practical elements

A warm and inviting colour, yellow suits boys and girls and is the • ideal colour for decorating a nursery in advance

Plastic boxes are stackable and easy to keep clean •

A roller blind lined with blackout fabric prevents baby waking up • in the summer months and is softened with lightweight curtains

A border of stencilled ducks picks out colours to coordinate with • accessories such as lampshades and storage boxes

1   2   3

stencilling a lampshade

easy

2 hours

Update a plain shade with a simple stencilled border to tie in with a new room scheme. If you have not stencilled before, practise first on a sheet of thick paper, to get a feel for the technique.

tools and materials

- small-duck-with-umbrella stencil template (see page 132)
- sheets of acetate
- craft knife or scalpel
- plain lampshade
- scissors
- stencil or low-tack masking tape
- stencil or emulsion paint in blue, yellow and reddish-orange
- old saucer
- stencil brush
- kitchen paper

1 Begin by making your stencil using the templates on page 132. Photocopy the templates then, again using the photocopier, copy them to the required size on to acetate. Using a craft knife or scalpel, carefully cut around each template.

2 Hold the stencil in place, towards the bottom edge of the lampshade, and secure it at the corners with small pieces of stencil or masking tape.

3 Pour a little paint into an old saucer and dip the tip of the stencil brush into the paint. It is important not to overload the brush, so dab off any excess paint on to a piece of kitchen paper. Begin to apply the paint to the lampshade by stippling the brush on to the stencil.

4 Carefully remove the stencil and tape. Before repositioning the stencil, work out the position of the rest of the motifs to ensure they are evenly spaced and mark with small pieces of masking tape. If you want the motifs very close together, it is important to let the paint dry first before repositioning the stencil, so as not to damage the new paint. Continue working around the shade until you reach where you started.

stencilling a border

easy

2 hours

It is surprisingly easy to liven up a plain wall with a cute border. Continue the yellow fluffy duck theme with this stencil. Either cut your own using our template (see page 131) or pick one up from a DIY retailer.

tools and materials

- **three-duck stencil template (see page 131)**
- **sheet of acetate**
- **craft knife or scalpel**
- **steel tape measure**
- **pencil**
- **scissors**
- **low-tack masking tape**
- **spirit level**
- **emulsion paint in yellow and reddish-orange**
- **2 old saucers**
- **2 stencil brushes**
- **kitchen paper**

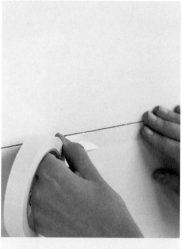

1 Begin by making your stencil, following the instructions in Step 1, page 32.

2 Decide the height at which you want the border and make a small pencil mark on the wall. Repeat this measurement at regular intervals along the wall or walls you are stencilling. Join up the pencil marks with lengths of low-tack masking tape. Mark a second parallel line in the same way to designate the width of the border. This will act as a guide when positioning the stencil. Use a spirit level to check that your taped lines are straight.

3 Starting near one corner of the room, align the stencil with the pre-taped lines and stick it to the wall using a small piece of masking tape at each corner.

4 Pour a small amount of yellow emulsion paint into an old saucer, dip the tip of the stencil brush in the paint and remove any excess on a piece of kitchen paper. Apply the paint with a stippling action to the main areas of the duck stencil.

5 Pour a little reddish-orange emulsion into another saucer and stipple on to the feet and beak parts of the stencil. Remove the masking tape from the stencil and carefully peel the stencil away from the wall. Repeat this process, stencilling along the wall, using the lengths of masking tape as a guide for positioning the stencil each time.

making a wall plaque

intermediate

3 hours

Decorate a wall with an easy-to-make plaque using inexpensive and readily available MDF. Create your own design or use our template of the umbrella-carrying duck in wellington boots to coordinate with the room's duck theme.

tools and materials

- pencil
- enlarged photocopy of duck template (see page 133) (optional)
- piece of 9mm (⁵⁄₁₆ in) MDF
- dust mask
- jigsaw and MDF blade
- household paintbrushes
- quick-drying wood primer
- emulsion paint in blue, yellow and reddish-orange
- permanent marker pen
- electric drill
- 2 wallplugs
- 2 screws and screwdriver

1 Start by sketching your chosen design directly on to the piece of MDF. Alternatively, cut out an enlarged photocopy of the template on page 133 and draw around this on to the MDF. Once you are happy with your design, fit the jigsaw with the MDF blade, put on the dust mask and cut out the shape, following the pencil lines as closely as possible.

2 Prime the plaque using quick-drying wood primer and leave to dry according to manufacturer's instructions. Paint the plaque using one or two coats of the emulsion paint, allowing the paint to dry thoroughly between coats and between applications of different colours.

3 Lastly, use the marker pen to outline the plaque and mark any features on your design.

4 Holding the plaque in position on the wall, drill a hole through the MDF and into the wall near the top and bottom of the plaque. Remove the plaque and insert wallplugs into the two holes in the wall. Note, the larger you make the plaque, the more screw supports it will require. Finish by screwing the plaque to the wall.

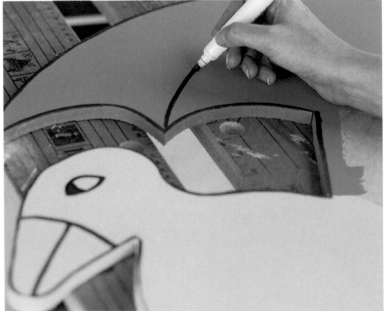

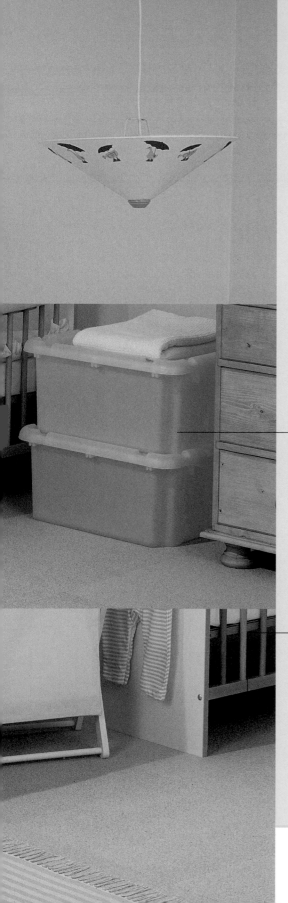

finishing touches

Babies accumulate an amazing amount of belongings and necessities very quickly, so versatile storage is a blessing. Look for colour-coordinated items or decorate them yourself.

● Soften a ceiling light with a stencilled uplighter. It won't be too bright and will also provide a lovely light to feed by. Don't forget to turn the stencil the right way so that the ducks aren't walking upside down!

● Colourful plastic boxes with lids are ideal for providing an extra hiding place for all those bits and pieces and can be neatly stacked in a corner or under the cot.

● Use carpet tiles for a soft but hard-wearing floor. They are easy to replace on a budget, tile by tile as necessary.

● Double up on space with a storage unit that is perfect for keeping toys and accessories neat and tidy but has a large enough surface to put a changing mat on top, so you won't need a separate changing area.

traditional nursery

In this simple scheme, traditional features and pretty details create a timeless look for a nursery. If you prefer pretty pastels to bold colours, you'll love this traditional-style nursery in cool minty greens, duck egg blues and pinks. Checks, ginghams and florals all make for a room that is both calm and relaxing for baby.

projects

- baby changing unit

- fabric-covered padded coat hangers

- handmade patchwork quilt

finishing touches

- fabric-covered armchair cushions

- painted mirror

- drawstring bag

- hanging peg rail

practical elements

Make the most of old furniture to create a scheme on a budget •

Light fabric curtains pair up with a roller blind to cut out light at night •

Pale-coloured walls form the basis of a scheme that is calm and relaxing •

storage
solutions

budget

room to
grow

1   2   3

making a baby changing unit

6 hours

Instead of buying purpose-made furniture for your new baby, customize an old chest of drawers to make the perfect changing unit. Make sure that it is a comfortable height for you, and deep enough to hold a changing mat.

tools and materials

- steel tape measure
- chest of drawers
- handsaw
- 3 pieces of planed timber, at least 10cm (4in) wide and 2cm (3/4in) thick
- medium-grade sandpaper and block
- hammer and panel pins
- length of wooden moulding to edge the planed timber
- wood glue
- household paintbrushes
- multi-surface primer
- satinwood or eggshell paint in cream or white
- changing mat

For the trays (optional):
- dust mask
- sheet of 6mm (1/4in) MDF
- 2 plywood garden trays

1 Measure the width and depth of the chest of drawers to determine the lengths of the three pieces of planed timber. You need one length along the back of the chest and two shorter lengths for the sides of the chest. Cut the timber and sand the sawn edges smooth. Nail the three pieces together with panel pins to form a three-sided frame for the top of the chest.

2 Cut three mitred strips of wooden moulding to fit the top edge of the framework and stick the moulding in place with wood glue. Leave to dry thoroughly then glue the three-sided framework to the top of the chest of drawers. Leave to dry.

3 If you wish to replace the top drawer with the garden trays, remove the top drawer and measure the inside dimensions of the chest. Wearing a dust mask, cut a piece of MDF to these dimensions to create a shelf on which the trays can sit. Secure it in place with panel pins.

4 Lightly sand the surface of the chest, and apply two coats of primer all over, including inside the top shelf as well as the wooden trays. Leave the first coat to dry completely before applying the second.

5 Finally, apply two coats of satinwood or eggshell paint, leaving the paint to dry thoroughly between coats. When the paint is completely dry, slide the wooden trays into the top shelf, and place the changing mat on top of the chest.

padding a coat hanger

easy

1 hour

Transform a plain plastic coat hanger into a pretty feature to show off some of your baby's favourite outfits. For a scented treat, you could also add some fragrance beads or a handful of dried lavender.

tools and materials

- quantity of wadding (see Step 1)
- scissors
- plastic clothes hanger
- needle and thread
- pencil and paper
- remnant of floral fabric
- dressmaker's pins
- length of ribbon

1 Cut a strip of wadding about 1m (1yd) long and 10cm (4in) wide, then wind it around the clothes hanger. Handstitch in place.

2 Draw around the hanger to create a paper template, then cut out two pieces of floral fabric to this size, allowing an extra 2cm (3/4in) of fabric for a seam allowance.

3 Pin the fabric to the padded hanger, then turn under the seam allowance all round and handstitch the fabric pieces together, pulling tightly around the wadding.

4 Tie a pretty ribbon around the hook of the hanger.

making a patchwork quilt

Easy

3 hours

Although a quilt is not suitable for a tiny baby's cot, this makes the perfect playmat. Beg or buy fabric remnants or ask your local fabric store for an old fabric swatch book – the samples are the perfect size.

tools and materials

- scissors
- selection of remnants of floral, patterned and gingham fabric
- dressmaker's pins
- sewing machine, needle and thread
- iron
- 1.3m (50in) gingham fabric to back quilt
- wadding

1 Cut eight squares of floral or patterned fabric, each measuring 30 x 30cm (12 x 12in), and eight squares the same size in gingham.

2 Pin, then machine or handstitch the squares together to make the front of the quilt, alternating the squares of gingham and floral fabric. Press all the seams flat.

3 Cut the gingham for the back of the quilt and the wadding to the same size as the front panel. Pin the backing and front panel together, right sides facing, then pin the wadding on top. Stitch around all four sides of the quilt, through all three layers, leaving a gap the size of one side of a square.

4 Turn the quilt the right side out, then handstitch the opening together before pressing flat. Finally, to create the quilted effect and help hold the wadding in place, topstitch over the seams joining each square.

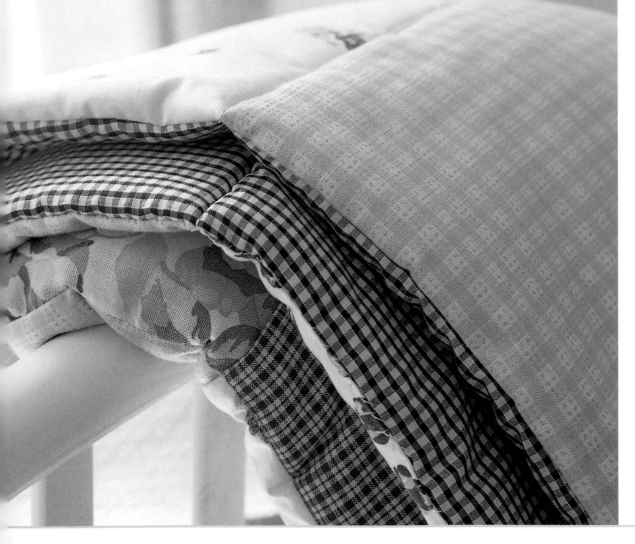

finishing touches

Stick to three or four coordinating fabrics and you will be able to use them in many ways around the nursery without worrying about clashing styles or unhappy pattern combinations.

• Make simple cushion covers in pretty florals and ginghams to add comfort to the room (see page 116 for instructions).

• Have a go at updating old mirror or picture frames with a coat of paint.

• Use other remnants of coordinating fabric to make drawstring bags (see page 46 for instructions), always useful for storing odds and ends.

• For a Shaker-style touch, make a peg rail from a length of planed timber with drawer knobs screwed in place.

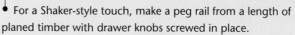

farmyard fun

Children's rooms should be fun, and a mural is a great idea. Leftover paint from other projects can be used and this farmyard scene provides lots of bold colours to pick out for accessories such as the curtains and bedlinen or pieces of furniture.

projects

- painted mural

- simple unlined curtains

- handy drawstring bag

finishing touches

- painted wardrobe

- toy box

- matching bedlinen

- cube storage unit

practical elements

A colourful mural stimulates children's imaginations •

Carpet tiles are a great idea for children's rooms – a single dirty • or damaged tile can be replaced quite easily

Neat storage tricks encourage children • to enjoy putting things away

Bedside table doubles as extra storage •

storage
solutions

budget

play area

43

farmyard fun

1   2   3

painting a farmyard mural

advanced

depends on design and size of room

The idea of painting a mural can be daunting, but even a simple design will thrill your child and you may surprise yourself by what you are able to achieve. Let them help – but be warned, it might get messy!

tools and materials

- farmyard/animals picture
- masking tape
- tracing paper
- pencil and ruler
- long, straight rule
- chalk
- selection of paintbrushes
- emulsion paint in various colours
- black marker pen (optional)

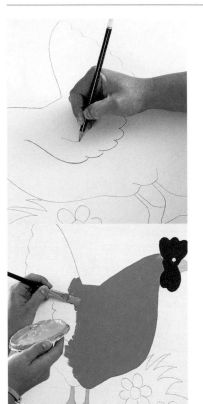

1 The first step is to decide on a design for the mural and find a picture you like. Take your chosen picture and tape a sheet of tracing paper over the top. Using a pencil and ruler, draw a grid over the whole picture. The more confident you are at drawing, the larger the grid squares can be, but if your picture is complicated a grid with more squares will make copying easier.

2 Next, using a long rule and chalk, copy the grid on to the wall. You will need to work out how large you wish the finished mural to be – for this mural each of the 5cm (2in) tracing paper grid squares corresponded to a 50cm (20in) square on the wall.

3 Now, using chalk or pencil, copy what is in each of your small squares on paper into the corresponding large squares on the wall.

4 Once you are happy with your design, paint the mural using emulsion paint. When the paint is dry, you can outline shapes using a black marker pen, if you wish.

making simple unlined curtains

easy

2 hours

Complete a room with a pair of coordinating curtains made in an afternoon. Unlined curtains are economical, practical, easy to make and ideal for rooms with little natural light.

tools and materials

- length of medium-weight fabric (measured to fit required window, see below)
- scissors
- tape measure
- dressmaker's pins
- sewing machine, needle and thread
- iron
- pinking shears (optional)
- length of two-pocket rufflette tape
- curtain hooks

---

1 Lay the curtain fabric on a cutting surface and cut the required number of lengths, ensuring the cutting lines are straight. For curtains with a standard heading the total fabric width required is normally 1½–2 times the length of the curtain pole or track.

2 If necessary, join panels together to create the correct width for each curtain. With right sides facing and raw edges aligned, pin, then tack panels together. Finally, machine stitch 1.5cm (⅝in) in from the raw edges. Remove the tacking stitches. Press the seams open and neaten

the raw edges with zigzag stitching, using pinking shears or by turning under and stitching a small hem.

3 To neaten the sides of each curtain, double-turn 3cm (1¼in) hems to hide the raw edges. Pin and tack in place. Press, then machine stitch and remove the tacking stitches.

4 Fold the top 5cm (2in) of each curtain to the wrong side, ensuring the edges are aligned, and press. Cut the heading tape into two lengths to match the width of each curtain. Folding the ends under to neaten, pin the tape in position on the wrong side of each curtain, 3cm (1¼in) down from the top edge so that the tape covers the turned-under raw edge. Secure the cords on each curtain at the end of the tape where the curtains will meet. Stitch the tape down carefully along its top and bottom edges, keeping close to the edge and sewing both lines in the same direction.

5 Lay the curtains flat. Measure from the top of each curtain down to the required length and mark with pins. Add on 10–15cm (4–6in) hem allowance and trim off any excess fabric. Fold the hem towards the wrong side, pin and press. Double turn the hem, pin, press and stitch in place.

6 Lastly, pull the loose cords of the heading tape to gather each curtain to the required width. Knot the cords and spread the gathers evenly. Insert the curtain hooks in the tape and hang the curtains.

making a drawstring bag

easy

1 hour

Make your own toy sacks using pillowcases and cord – you'll find them really roomy for storing all sorts of toys and other bits and pieces. Leave them plain, stencil with fabric paints or transfer a picture (see page 29).

(see page 29).

tools and materials

- pillowcase
- tape measure
- dressmaker's pins
- sewing machine, needle and thread
- large safety pin
- 1m (1yd) white cord

1 Take a pillowcase and turn under a 4cm (1½in) border at the open end. Pin in place then machine or handstitch to form a casing for the cord, leaving a 2cm (¾in) gap at one of the side seams.

2 Attach the safety pin to one end of the length of cord and thread the pin through the casing in the pillowcase. To finish, knot the two ends of the cord together and trim.

finishing touches

Using the colours of your mural to guide you, limit the rest of the room to just one or two key colours, or the impact of the mural will be lost. Here, lime green and dusky blue link the scheme.

A junk shop wardrobe can be given a new lease of life with a coat of paint and a part of the mural picked out as a detail and painted on the doors.

A toy box is another useful item in a child's room – just throw everything in at the end of the day. This too can be painted to match the colour scheme. Use satinwood or egg shell as they are wipeable.

There are lots of great bedlinen designs to choose from. This pretty gingham set is a good foil against the mural on the walls and is plain on the reverse side. Mix lime with blue for a smart look.

Cube storage is all the rage and often available ready for you to paint or stain yourself to coordinate with the rest of the colour scheme.

nautical air

Capture a sense of fun by giving a bedroom a nautical touch. Fabric is a key element for providing colour and pattern and the theme for this room started with a range of ready-made coordinating bedding, curtains and lampshades. A simple makeover of the bed – one of the most important items of furniture in any bedroom – will have your child always wanting to go to bed on time.

projects

- lighthouse headboard

- nautical picture frames

- rope-strung wooden shelves

finishing touches

- nautical lampshade

- peg rails

- colourwashed wooden floor

- coordinating bedlinen

practical elements

Small hooks from which to hang bags help to keep things tidy •

Several tones of one colour is a sure-fire decorating trick. • Here, blues blend beautifully within the room

An ordinary bed has been given the lighthouse treatment with the • addition of a clever MDF headboard painted in bold primary colours

Stencilled sea creature motifs take only minutes to do and have • been scattered at random around the room to great effect

budget

helping
hand

nautical air

1 **2** **3**

making a lighthouse headboard

advanced

4–5 hours

Any little boy will love this lighthouse headboard made from MDF. If a lighthouse doesn't suit, how about a pirate ship?

tools and materials

- steel tape measure
- sheet of 18mm (1¹/₁₆in) MDF
- ruler
- lighthouse template (see page 134)
- pencil and eraser
- workbench and clamps
- jigsaw and MDF blade
- dust mask
- assorted household paintbrushes and sponge
- MDF primer
- emulsion paint in red, white, yellow, light and dark grey
- permanent marker pen
- acrylic varnish
- electric drill
- 2 wallplugs
- 2 screws and screwdriver

1 Measure the width of the bed base and add 10cm (4in). Decide on a height for the headboard, the one pictured here measured 120cm (48in). Lay the sheet of MDF on the floor and mark out these dimensions and the centre vertical.

2 Using the lighthouse template on page 134 for reference, draw the outline directly on to the MDF. If you make a mistake, simply rub out the lines and start again.

3 Secure the sheet of MDF to your workbench using the clamps. Wearing the dust mask, carefully cut around the shape with the jigsaw.

4 Prime the headboard front and back using special MDF primer. Leave to dry thoroughly.

5 Paint the board with white emulsion and leave to dry before completing the details on the lighthouse with red and yellow paint and marker pen. Tip a little of each grey and a little white emulsion paint on to a dinner plate. Wet the sponge and squeeze dry. Dip the sponge in the grey paints and sponge all over the rock to give a mottled appearance. Keep sponging with a mixture of grey and white until the whole rock is painted. Don't forget to sponge the edges of the board as well for a really professional finish. When the paintwork is completely dry, apply two coats of acrylic varnish, leaving it to dry thoroughly between coats.

6 Drill two holes through the headboard, one on each side edge about half way down. Hold the headboard against the wall at the top of the bed and mark the holes on the wall. Drill holes into the wall and push a wallplug into each hole. Screw the headboard into the wall and check that it is firmly attached to the wall before pushing the bed into place.

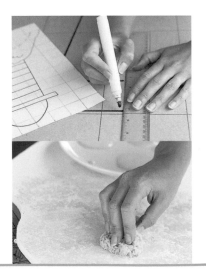

customizing picture frames

easy

1 hour

Make these nautical themed picture frames for a room inspired by the ocean. Collecting the shells could be part of the fun. Get your children to paint some doodles and pictures to go inside the frames.

tools and materials

- matt emulsion paint in blue
- old newspapers
- household paintbrush
- 2 unvarnished pine picture frames
- length of jute rope 5 times the height of the frames
- steel tape measure
- all-purpose glue
- rope knots and seashells, to decorate (optional)

1 Since the nautical look relies heavily on wood, let the natural grain of the wood show through by diluting the matt emulsion paint with water – a colourwash of half water and half paint is just right.

2 Spread your work surface with newspaper and give the back and front of each frame a coat of the colourwash, brushing the paint along the grain of the wood. Lean the frames on something while they dry to keep the backs off the newspaper.

3 Replace the pictures and glass in the frames and lay the frames face down. Glue one end of the rope to each bottom corner of one frame, before gluing the rope up the sides of the frame. Position the second frame 5cm (2in) above the first and continue gluing the rope up the sides of the second frame. You will be left with a hanging loop of rope at the top.

4 When glue is dry turn the frames over and decorate with rope knots and seashells if desired.

making rope shelves

easy

2 hours

These simple wooden shelves will add a nautical theme to any little sailor's bedroom. They will not be sturdy enough for heavy items, but are perfect for little seaside mementoes and collectibles.

tools and materials

- small quantity of emulsion paint in blue
- old tablespoon
- old cup or bowl
- household paintbrush
- two 50 x 10 x 2.5cm (20 x 4 x 1in) lengths of planed pine
- steel tape measure
- pencil
- electric drill, plus appropriate size bit for wallplugs
- 2m (2¹/₄yd) natural rope or jute
- 6 wallplugs and screws (suitable for your type of walls)
- 2 large cup hooks
- 4 mirror plates 25mm (1in) deep
- 4 self tapping screws to fit mirror plates

1 Measure 10cm (4in) from the ends of each shelf and make a pencil mark in the centre. Using a bit for drilling wood, drill a large hole at each of the four marked positions, just big enough for the rope to pass through – sand the holes smooth.

2 Dilute the emulsion paint to make a colourwash by mixing 1 tablespoon of emulsion with 1 tablespoon of water. If you want a thinner wash just stir in a little more water. Brush the colourwash evenly all over the two shelves. Rest each shelf on a can at either end and leave to dry. Screw 2 mirror plates to the back of each shelf using the self tapping screws.

3 Cut the rope into two equal lengths, knot the end of one piece and thread it upwards through a drilled hole in one of the shelves. Repeat using the second length of rope, threading through the other hole in the same shelf. Now make a knot a little higher up the rope where you want the top shelf to sit and repeat on the other side in exactly the same position. Thread the rope upwards through the holes in the top shelf. Bear in mind that you may have to adjust the positions of these second knots slightly to ensure that the top shelf is level.

4 Make a loop at the top of each length of rope, and secure with a knot. Hold the shelves against the wall and make two pencil marks to indicate the position of the cup hooks on which to hang the shelves. Then drill holes in the wall for the wallplugs to take the cup hooks. Screw the hooks in place and hang the shelves from the loops at the top of each piece of rope.

5 In pencil, mark the position of the screw holes for the mirror plates on the wall. Remove the shelves. Drill holes in the wall for the wallplugs. Re-hang the shelves and fix the screws in place, screwing through each mirror plate.

finishing touches

Carry through the nautical theme first inspired by the bedlinen and curtains with other oceanic touches. Sea motifs are easy to find, and a colourwash gives wood a bleached, driftwood look.

• Coordinating soft furnishings are a great way of finishing a room and will really tie a new scheme together.

• Peg rails make the perfect finishing touch in kids' rooms as they are ideal for hanging up toy bags and clothes and help to keep the floor free from clutter. They look great at picture rail height but you could also put them lower down so that toddlers can reach the hooks.

• Give a sanded solid pine wooden floor a colourwash of diluted paint (1 part emulsion to 2 parts water). Apply with a large paintbrush or sponge and seal with floor varnish when dry.

• Stencils or transfer stickers of seashells, fish and starfish add to the nautical theme. Children can help with these and will enjoy getting involved in decorating their own room. Also include bedlinen and curtains with a nautical theme.

pretty in pink

Little girls tend to love the colour pink. However, if you're not keen on colours that are too bright, opt instead for this fresh-looking and very pretty pink bedroom using 1950s-style florals, soft pinks and only a hint of fuchsia with pale pink paint on the walls, a white painted floor and offcuts of floral wallpaper.

project

- daisy-stamped mini cabinet

finishing touches

- daisy-stamped wooden chest

- pretty bedhead

- bold colours

- wallpaper wardrobe

practical elements

Sanded and painted floors offer durability and are easy to maintain •

A retro spin on every girl's favourite colour •

Combine pastel-coloured gingham with feminine •
floral patterns for a cosy, traditional feel

specially
for girls

budget

play area

room to
grow

55

pretty in pink

1

2

3

decorating a mini cabinet

easy

2 hours

Little girls love little boxes, so why not make a handy storage chest for small odds and ends by customizing a mini cabinet with drawers? Ideal for all kinds of hairbands and accessories and the perfect way to keep a room free from clutter.

tools and materials

- mini wooden cabinet
- household paintbrush
- wood primer
- emulsion paint in fuchsia pink and white
- old teaspoon and saucer
- small roller
- daisy stamp
- newspaper or kitchen paper
- acrylic varnish

1 Remove the drawers and prime the outside of the cabinet and the drawer fronts.

2 When the primer is dry apply two coats of fuchsia pink emulsion, allowing the paint to dry thoroughly between coats.

3 Put a teaspoon of white emulsion in an old saucer and spread it thinly using the back of the spoon. Dip the roller in the paint, remove the excess then roll it across the daisy stamp. Practise stamping on a wad of newspaper or kitchen paper. When you are happy with your technique recoat the stamp with paint and position it centrally on one of the drawer fronts. Press down firmly and then carefully lift the stamp away. Stamp each drawer and leave to dry.

4 To finish the cabinet, apply two coats of acrylic varnish, allowing it to dry between coats.

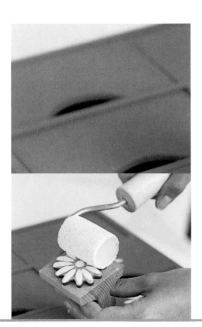

finishing touches

The effect of many different patterns and styles can easily get messy, but keeping within the pink and white colour scheme will unify the design and link the elements together.

• Transform existing pieces of furniture like this wooden chest with pretty daisy stamps.

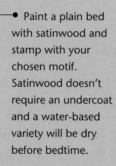

• Paint a plain bed with satinwood and stamp with your chosen motif. Satinwood doesn't require an undercoat and a water-based variety will be dry before bedtime.

• Use the boldest colour in your colour scheme in small doses, like the fuchsia pink of this mirror frame.

• Complement the room scheme by pasting offcuts of floral wallpaper on to cupboard doors and using remnants of fabric to make cushion covers (see page 116 for instructions).

jungle bedroom

A colourful mural transforms a child's bedroom into a magical room with a fun jungle theme. With a bit of imagination you can change a boring bedroom into a jungle den with a menagerie of animals and birds.

projects

- hanging toy tidy

- hand-print pictures

- jungle clock

finishing touches

- wooden shelving

- fun storage ideas

- animal soft furnishings

- jungle wall mural

practical elements

A neutral carpet provides a contrast to the busy walls •
and can easily be worked into future schemes

The jungle theme offers plenty of scope for •
imaginative ideas and encourages children to
become involved in creating the scheme

A generous toy chest is invaluable in children's rooms •

59

jungle bedroom

1   2   3

making a hanging toy tidy

intermediate

3 hours

This easy-to-make toy tidy in hardwearing denim has pockets that are just the job for books, crayons and toys. Hang on the back of the door – it will help encourage your kids to tidy up!

- tape measure
- scissors
- length of denim (see Step 1)
- sewing machine, needle and thread
- dressmaker's pins
- iron
- handsaw
- medium wooden dowelling
- 2 screw hooks
- string or ribbon

1 Measure the width of the bedroom door. Cut a rectangle of denim to fit, allowing extra fabric for a hem on each side edge and for a 4cm (1½in) casing for the dowelling at the top and bottom. Hem the side edges. At the top and bottom of the panel, turn over a 4cm (1½in) hem to the back and stitch in place.

2 Decide on the size and number of your pockets, then cut strips of denim 30cm (12in) longer than the width of the back panel and as wide as your pocket height, plus seam allowances. Hem the long edges of each strip.

3 Pin the strips lengthways across the back panel, matching the middle of each long strip to the centre of the panel. Turn under the short ends of the strips to neaten and stitch to the side edges of the back panel. Create the pockets by sewing vertical seams at equal distances along each strip. Neatly gather the excess material at the bottom corner of each pocket, pin in place then machine along the entire length of each row to seal the bottom of the pockets. Press well.

4 Cut two pieces of wooden dowelling to the width of the finished back panel. Insert a length of dowelling into the channels at the top and bottom of the back panel. Screw a hook into each end of the dowelling in the top channel and tie a length of ribbon or string to each hook by which to hang the pocket tidy.

hand-printing pictures

very easy

30 minutes

Kids can have fun making these bright prints to hang on the wall. Simple hand-prints or foot prints are satisfying, or they can be the basis for fantasy 'hand animals' – just add eyes, beaks, claws, scales . . .

tools and materials

- wooden picture frame
- household paintbrushes
- emulsion paint
- acrylic varnish
- water-based paint for printing
- shallow tray
- cartridge paper
- scissors

1 Start by giving the frame a coat of emulsion paint and leaving it to dry thoroughly. Then apply two coats of acrylic varnish, leaving it to dry well between coats.

2 Pour a little water-based paint into a shallow tray and supervise your child as they dip their hands into the paint, then press firmly on to a clean sheet of paper. Make sure they wash their hands immediately with soap and water.

3 Using the picture frame as a guide, cut the paper to a suitable size and mount it into the frame.

making a coordinating clock

intermediate

2 hours

It's easy to make a clock that suits your bedroom scheme. Here we have decorated the clock with paw-print potato stamps. Another plus is that it's great for teaching kids to tell the time too!

tools and materials

- pencil
- piece of 6mm (¹/₄in) MDF
- dinner plate
- jigsaw and MDF blade
- dust mask
- medium-grade sandpaper and block
- household paintbrush
- multi-surface primer
- matt emulsion paint in cream and brown
- kitchen knife and craft knife or scalpel
- 2 potatoes
- felt-tip pen
- paw print template (see page 135) (optional)
- kitchen paper
- permanent marker pen
- electric drill
- clock mechanism and hands

1 Draw a circle on a piece of 6mm (¹/₄ in) MDF, using a dinner plate as a guide. Fit the jigsaw with the MDF blade, put on the dust mask and cut out the circle, following the pencil line. Sand the edges lightly.

2 Apply two coats of multi-surface primer to the MDF circle, allowing the primer to dry thoroughly between coats. Then paint on at least two coats of cream matt emulsion, again leaving the paint to dry well between coats.

3 When the clock face is completely dry, it is ready for stamping with paw prints or a design of your choice. Halve the potatoes using a sharp knife. Using a felt-tip pen, draw your chosen shape (see the paw print template on page 135 for reference, or make up your own) on the cut potato, which will be wet. Using a craft knife or scalpel, cut downwards around the shape following the pen outline, then slice carefully into the side of the potato to meet the vertical cuts. Remove the excess potato around the relief you have created. Pat the cut surface of potato dry with kitchen paper.

4 Smear the potato stamp evenly with a little brown emulsion paint then press it carefully on the clock face to decorate. When the paint is dry write the numbers on the clock face with a permanent marker pen. Finally, drill a hole in the centre of the circle and attach the clock mechanism, according to the manufacturer's instructions.

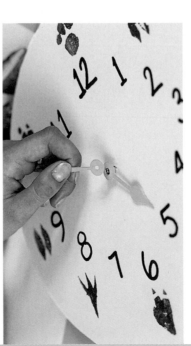

finishing touches

From faux fur floor cushions and cuddly toys to travel posters and jungle-print bedding, there is no end to the finishing touches that will bring the call of the wild to this bedroom.

Add wooden shelving, chests and underbed boxes to keep clutter under control. Buy ready-to-paint furniture and shelves and paint it to tie in with the new scheme.

Giving your child lots of fun storage ideas will encourage them to tidy away their toys.

Look out for animal cushion covers, bedside rugs and even sleeping bags with a wild animal theme. This zebra cushion looks the part and can be used on the floor to provide extra seating.

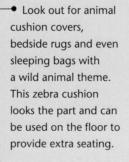

Draw a fascinating mural around the room based on your child's favourite animals (see page 44 for instructions).

room to share

A brother and sister sharing the same space need little areas that they feel are their own – like the pinboards and storage boxes – as well as areas for them to share, such as the padded bench and blackboard. The aim, too, is to organize the chaotic clutter of toys, inject colour and generally make the room feel more like a den rather than a toy box!

projects

- bench seat that doubles as storage

- an instant blackboard

- tab-top curtains

- a simple box shelf

finishing touches

- dyed bedlinen

- funky furniture

- cork notice board

practical elements

Meets the needs of a brother and sister who share a room •

Each child is allocated their own personal space •

Maximum storage space is doubly necessary • when two are sharing

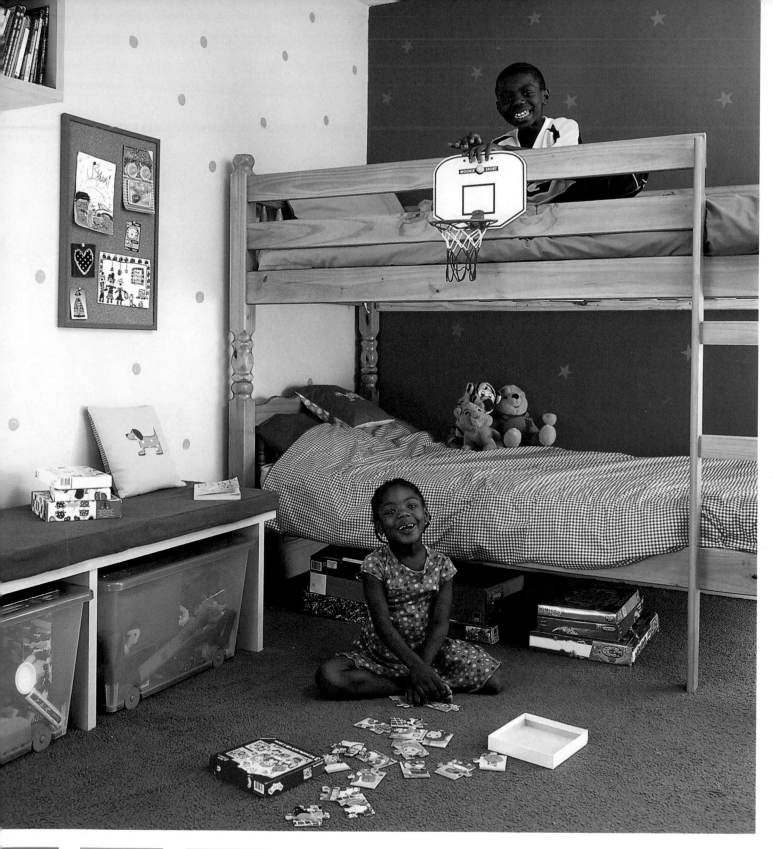

storage
solutions

budget

play area

65

room to share

1   2   3

making a storage seat

advanced

4–5 hours

Your kids will love this comfy seat that doubles as a handy storage chest. Easy to make, this seat can be painted with leftover paint and covered with cushions to tie in with your colour scheme.

1 Working on the top piece, draw a pencil line 6.5cm (2½in) in from either short end. Drilling along the pencil lines, drill 3 holes down, at 5, 20 and 35cm (2, 8 and 14in) intervals and countersink.

2 Drill 3 holes using the same measurements as above along the centre and down one side of each of the two side pieces. Repeat for the central support – drilling holes in the 3.75cm (15in) long side. Apply wood glue along each joint and screw the three vertical supports to the seat top.

3 Fix the back of the bench in place, in between the side pieces and to the centre piece, in the same way as above, using 9 screws.

4 Apply one or two coats of multi-surface primer to the bench, allowing the primer to dry thoroughly between coats. Then paint on two coats of matt emulsion, again leaving the paint to dry well between coats.

5 To make the cushion for the seat, make a cover for the foam by wrapping the jersey cotton around the foam and sewing the side and top seams together neatly by hand. Put two storage crates in each alcove, ready to be filled with toys!

SAFETY NOTE: For extra safety attach battens to the wall and screw the bench to the battens.

creating a blackboard

easy

1 hour

Paint a blackboard directly on to the wall in a child's bedroom – it will keep them amused for hours and they won't get into trouble for writing on this particular wall! The back of the bedroom door is another good location.

tools and materials

- masking tape
- steel tape measure
- spirit level
- household paintbrush
- blackboard paint, regular or aerosol

For the chalk ledge (optional):
- small strip of painted wood
- electric drill
- wallplugs
- screws and screwdriver

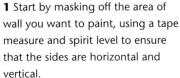

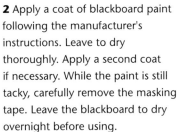

1 Start by masking off the area of wall you want to paint, using a tape measure and spirit level to ensure that the sides are horizontal and vertical.

2 Apply a coat of blackboard paint following the manufacturer's instructions. Leave to dry thoroughly. Apply a second coat if necessary. While the paint is still tacky, carefully remove the masking tape. Leave the blackboard to dry overnight before using.

3 To make a ledge for the chalk, hold a small strip of painted wood against the wall near the bottom of the blackboard. Use the spirit level to check it is horizontal. Drill through the strip at each end into the wall. Insert wallplugs in the wall then screw the batten in place.

making tab-top curtains

Simple tab-tops are one of the easiest and most inexpensive curtains you can make. They are easy to open and close, making them ideal for children's rooms. Don't forget to paint the pole to coordinate.

tools and materials

- **length of voile or other lightweight fabric for the curtains (see Step 1), plus extra for tabs; 30cm (12in) of 122cm (48in) fabric will be enough for 12 tabs**
- **dressmaker's pins**
- **iron**
- **sewing machine, needle and thread**
- **scissors**

1 Measure your window to determine the quantity of fabric required. You want a total fabric width of 1½ x the width of the window x the length of the window plus 10cm (4in) for turnings for each curtain. Decide whether your window requires one or two curtains.

2 Turn under a 2cm (³⁄₄in) hem at the top and bottom of each curtain, pin and press. Turn over a further 3cm (1¼in), pin and press again. Machine stitch the hems in place, removing the pins as you work. For the sides of the curtains you may be able to leave the selvage edges (the edge of a length of cloth that doesn't unravel) as they are if they are neat. Otherwise turn under a 1cm (³⁄₈in) hem down the side of each curtain, pin, press and stitch in place.

3 Lay one of the curtains on a flat work surface with the top of the curtain nearest you. Position a pin at either end of the top edge of the curtain. Measure the gap between the pins and position a pin roughly every 20cm (8in). Adjust until the

spacing between the pins is equal. You will need to cut a tab for every pin, and cut the same number of tabs for the other curtain.

4 Cut the tabs from the excess fabric, each tab measuring 30 x 10cm (12 x4in). Fold each tab in half lengthways, right sides facing, press and pin. Stitch down one long edge and across one short side of each tab. Trim the fabric. Turn the tabs right side out, smooth flat and press. Turn in the raw edges of each tab and topstitch to finish.

5 Fold the tabs in half and pin to the top of curtains at the marked positions. The tabs should overlap the curtain, front and back, by about 3cm (1¼in). Topstitch in place and secure the stitching.

making a box shelf

intermediate

4–5 hours

Box shelves are perfect for displaying favourite bits and pieces such as books and miniature toys, and they are also very simple to make. Each child can have their own, to avoid squabbles.

Variation For an even simpler style of box shelf, make a four-sided open 'box', omitting the back piece. Fix it to the wall using strong brass picture plates screwed to the wooden frame.

1 Decide on the dimensions for your box shelf and cut two identical pieces of MDF for the sides, two identical pieces for the top and bottom and one piece for the back, large enough to back the rectangle made by the other four pieces.

2 Hold the back piece level against the wall (check with a spirit level) and drill two holes through the MDF and into the wall. Remove the MDF and insert wallplugs into the drilled holes in the wall.

3 Now assemble the box using wood glue and panel pins. First join the four side pieces of the box then apply wood glue to their top edges. Press the back piece on top and hammer in panel pins to secure.

4 Paint the box with MDF primer and leave to dry thoroughly. Apply one or two coats of emulsion, leave to dry and finish off with two coats of acrylic varnish. When the box shelf is finished hold it against the wall and screw tightly in place.

finishing touches

Rather than just leaving the walls a flat colour, add a stamped design in a slightly paler or darker shade of paint. Use a purpose-made rubber stamp or make random blobs with a small sponge.

• Breathe new life into faded bedlinen with a machine dye in coordinating colours (any two distinctive colours that sit well together). This will help distinguish each child's bedding, toy store and personal areas.

• An alternative to painting furniture is to cover it with sticky-backed plastic – it takes half the time and leaves no mess! Remove any handles and measure the front of the drawers. Cut the sticky-backed plastic to size, peel off the backing and stick it on the front of the drawers, then replace the handles.

• Give each child a cork notice board on which they can pin their own pictures, invitations or special souvenirs. Boards come in several sizes and you can paint the frame in the room's colours.

vibrant study

Children's rooms become more important to them as they get older and need a room for sleeping, studying and playing, so make their room bright and fun by using lively colours they have chosen themselves and adding fun accessories. Allocating a corner in which to study is a good way of getting children to enjoy working and keeps everything in one place.

practical elements

A bold colour scheme will keep its appeal as children get older •

Colour-coordinated magazine files and • storage boxes provide a funky look

Laminate flooring is durable and easy to clean. • It also provides a neutral background if you wish to change the colour scheme of the room later on

Blinds are easy for children to use •

study area

room to grow

play area

budget

1   2   3

making an alcove desk

advanced

6 hours

Making a study area in an alcove is a great way of using space. The surface can be shaped for a more unusual look and the space above makes a good framework for shelves. A fun area to work in will hopefully encourage more study!

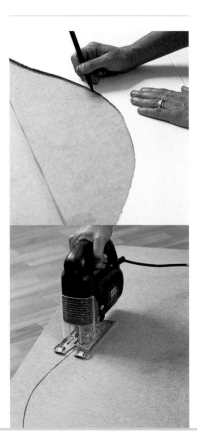

1 Measure the space available for the desk and make a template out of stiff card to the shape that you like. Use the template to draw the outline on to a sheet of MDF. Once you are happy with your design, fit the jigsaw with the MDF blade, put on the dust mask and cut out the shape, following the pencil line as closely as possible.

2 Decide on the ideal height for your desk – most desks stand 70–75cm (28–30in) high – and mark the height on the wall. Cut the timber into three to make three battens to fit the walls of the alcove in a 'U' shape. Use a spirit level to check they are level, fix the battens to the wall by using an electric drill then inserting wallplugs and screwing the battens in place. Sit the desk top on top of the battens and screw it down into them, countersinking the screw holes. (If the desk top is very long and heavy, you may decide that you want an additional vertical support at the front edge of the desk top.)

3 Fill the screw holes with fine surface filler, then paint the desk top with one or two coats of primer. Finish it with two coats of a satinwood, eggshell or gloss paint for a durable finish.

customizing a lampshade

easy

1 hour

Stripes of coloured ribbon are all it takes to make an ordinary lampshade look really special. It's a simple idea that can lead to all sorts of creative variations, suitable for bedlinen and cushions for example.

tools and materials

- **tape measure**
- **cylindrical plain-coloured lampshade**
- **scissors**
- **ribbon in chosen colour and width**
- **all-purpose glue**

1 Use the tape measure to measure the circumference of the lampshade. Add 2cm (³/₄in) to this measurement and cut three lengths of ribbon to this length.

2 Apply a little glue along the length of one of the ribbons. Starting at the seam of the shade, near the bottom edge, wrap the ribbon around the shade pressing it in place as you work. Check that the ribbon is equal distance from the edge as you go around the lampshade. When you reach the end of the ribbon turn under the raw end to neaten and overlap it neatly over the beginning of the ribbon. Leave the glue to dry before repeating the process with the remaining two lengths of ribbon.

giving furniture a makeover

intermediate

6 hours

For funky furniture on a budget, why not give an old chest of drawers a face-lift by painting it in a colour to match your scheme and then adding new drawer knobs? Check out your local car boot sale and junk shop for a bargain.

tools and materials

- old chest of drawers
- screwdriver
- electric sander or medium-grade sandpaper and block
- damp cloth
- household paintbrush
- quick-drying wood primer
- satinwood paint in vibrant orange
- new drawer knobs

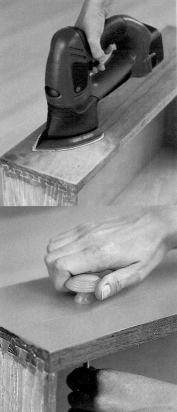

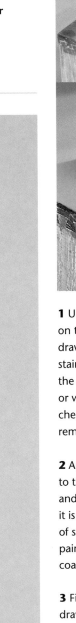

1 Unscrew the old knobs or handles on the chest and remove the drawers. Remove the old finish or stain, paint or varnish by sanding the chest and drawer fronts by hand or with an electric sander. Wipe the chest down with a damp cloth to remove dust.

2 Apply quick-drying wood primer to the outside of the chest of drawers and the front of each drawer. When it is completely dry, apply two coats of satinwood paint, allowing the paint to dry thoroughly between coats.

3 Finally, attach new knobs to the drawers, screwing them in place from the back of each drawer front.

finishing touches

Keeping pattern to a minimum means you can make the most of bright, contrasting colours. Accessories in lime green, orange, blue, red and bright yellow all combine cheerfully.

• Blue plastic storage boxes and crates work perfectly with the funky, bright colours of the room and are ideal for storing all sorts of bits and pieces. Line shelves with them, put them in the bottom of a wardrobe or simply stack them in a corner of the room.

• Make a feature of a blocked-up fireplace by painting the wall with blackboard paint (see page 68) – you will have a great place for your child to express artistic talent!

• New bedlinen instantly livens up a new room and white always looks fresh. You could add appliqué shapes to plain bedding in colours to pick out accessories. Painting wooden bed frames will also tie them into the room's colour scheme.

sunshine bedroom

The classic wrought-iron bed is a timeless design that will comfortably take your child from tot to teen. Combine it with pastel pink and yellow colours, pink appliquéd gingham curtains and bedding and wooden storage pieces painted to match the colour scheme to create a really pretty bedroom.

projects

- customized mini storage chest

- decorated underbed storage boxes

- jazzed-up mirror

finishing touches

- gingham cushion covers

- wooden ornament shelf

- gingham picture frames

- daisy lampshade

- painted alcove

practical elements

Clever storage tricks are designed to encourage tidiness •

Strong colours provide a good backdrop • for the white wrought-iron bed

A feature is made of the wall alcove by • positioning the bed and bedside cabinet within it and painting it a contrasting colour to the other walls

Peg rails provide extra hanging space for knick-knacks •

specially for girls

storage solutions

room to grow

helping hand

play area

79

sunshine bedrooms

1 2 3

creating a mini bedside cabinet

intermediate

3 hours

With the addition of legs to raise its height, this mini CD storage unit makes a perfect child's bedside cabinet and the drawers are just the right size for storing socks, underwear and toys.

tools and materials

- 6-drawer CD storage unit
- household paintbrush
- emulsion paint in white, pink and yellow
- daisy stamp (can be bought from any good DIY retailer)
- craft knife or scalpel
- rubber squeegee blade
- clean plastic container or old saucer
- old spoon
- acrylic scumble glaze
- kitchen paper
- matt acrylic varnish
- carved legs
- hot-glue gun and wood glue sticks

1 Give the outside of the cabinet and all six drawers a coat of white emulsion paint and allow to dry.

2 Paint two drawer fronts in pink and then another in yellow emulsion. Leave these to dry before stamping each with a daisy in a contrasting colour.

3 Use a sharp craft knife or scalpel to cut notches out of a rubber squeegee blade. In a plastic container mix a glaze of one part yellow emulsion to two parts scumble glaze and paint it over the remaining drawer fronts and cabinet. Before the glaze has time to dry, drag the squeegee carefully through the glaze to produce stripes. Use kitchen paper to wipe any excess glaze from the squeegee at the end of each stroke.

4 Allow the glaze to dry thoroughly according to manufacturer's instructions, then apply a coat of matt acrylic varnish over the painted cabinet and drawer fronts.

5 Paint the carved wooden legs with a couple of coats of yellow emulsion, allowing the paint to dry thoroughly between coats. Then apply a coat of matt acrylic varnish. Once dry, stick the legs to the four corners of the cabinet using wood glue sticks in a hot-glue gun.

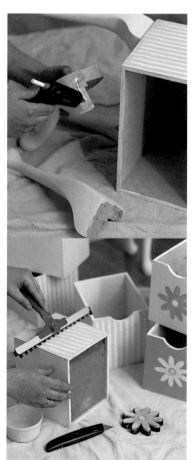

painting underbed storage boxes

easy

2 hours

Keep the clutter under control with the help of these colourful storage boxes that fit neatly under the bed. When full they are easier to move than one big box. Ideal for toys, books or clothes.

tools and materials

- household paintbrush
- quick-drying wood primer
- wooden storage boxes
- emulsion paint in yellow and pink
- daisy stamp
- clear all-purpose glue
- clear glass beads
- acrylic varnish
- self-adhesive furniture protector pads or castors and screws

1 Start by applying a coat of quick-drying wood primer to the boxes and leave to dry thoroughly. Then paint the insides of the boxes with pink emulsion and the outsides with yellow paint. Apply a second coat of each colour if necessary when the first coats are dry.

2 When the top coat is dry, decorate the front of the boxes by stamping them with a daisy design smeared with pink emulsion. To finish, stick a clear glass bead in the centre of each flower.

3 Finish with two coats of acrylic varnish, allowing the varnish to dry between coats. This will help give the boxes a hardwearing finish. If you have wooden floors, turn the boxes upside down and stick furniture protector pads in the corners to help prevent them scratching the floor. If you have carpets, screw small castors on the underside of the boxes, one in each corner.

Variation

To achieve a gingham effect on the box fronts adapt a rubber squeegee blade, make up a glaze and paint stripes, following the instructions for Step 3 of the mini bedside cabinet (see page 80). To complete the effect, wait for the first stripes to dry thoroughly, apply another coat of glaze then pull the squeegee across in the opposite direction from the first stripes to create the check look of gingham. Yellow and pink and blue and green are winning colour combinations.

jazzing up a plain mirror

easy

30 minutes

Add the finishing touch to your child's room by customizing a mirror with pretty coloured gem stones or glass beads. It's easy to do and is a great way to encourage your child's creativity. Try this design on a picture frame as well.

tools and materials

- circular mirror
- newspaper
- coloured plastic gemstones or glass beads
- clear all-purpose glue

1 Make sure the mirror is spotlessly clean. Lay it on a flat work surface and protect the surrounding area with newspaper.

2 Decide on the pattern to make with the gemstones or beads and lay them on the mirror, experimenting until you are happy with your design. Apply a little glue to the back of each gem or bead and glue in place following manufacturer's instructions.

3 Leave the glue to dry completely before hanging the mirror.

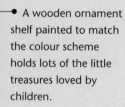

finishing touches

Little girls love everything to coordinate, so choose bedlinen and curtains from the same range. If you are good at sewing you could even have a go at embroidery or appliqué.

- Make simple cushion covers in pretty florals and ginghams to coordinate with the room (see page 116 for instructions).

- A wooden ornament shelf painted to match the colour scheme holds lots of the little treasures loved by children.

- Give plain picture frames a fun new look by painting them white and mounting designer postcards framed with gingham fabric. Hang from a peg rail using lengths of gingham ribbon.

- Dress up a simple calico lampshade by gluing silk daisies randomly over its surface.

- Add interest to a plain alcove by painting it in a contrasting colour. Then fix up a peg rail and hang pictures and toys from the pegs.

soccer
mania

projects

- soccer uplighters

- soccer pitch floor

- roller blind stencilled
  with soccer motifs

finishing touches

- fireplace goal

- changing room effect

- drawstring bags

Soccer fanatic in the family? Their bedroom needn't be plastered with posters and souvenirs. Instead of using busy soccer patterns on bedding, curtains or walls, why not use team colours to reflect support? With a little forethought you can create a room that will be fun to live with, and easy to change when the time comes.

practical elements

The look is fun for all boys and girls and easy to adapt •

Durable and easy to clean, the laminate flooring •
is tough enough to take the knocks. White sticky tape lines
transform it instantly into a pitch

The look of the dressing room is effectively recreated •

An original fireplace makeover transforms what might have been •
an out-of-place feature

Colour scheme based on your child's favourite team's strip •

budget

room to grow

play area

85

soccer mania

making soccer uplighters

easy

1 hour

Complete a soccer themed room with soccer inspired uplighters – they're practical, they're easy to make, and they're sure to score highly with any soccer fan! They're available from most large DIY retailers.

tools and materials

- pentagon and hexagon templates (see page 136)
- pencil
- thin card
- scissors
- 2 plaster uplighters
- newspaper
- small paintbrush
- emulsion or craft paint in black
- permanent black marker pen

---

1 Copy the pentagon and hexagon templates onto thin card and cut out.

2 Sit the uplighters on a sheet of newspaper. Using the card templates draw pentagons surrounded by hexagons all over each uplighter to represent the pattern on a soccer ball. You will need to wedge the uplighter up at an angle to do the part-hexagons around the curving bottom edge.

3 Using a small paintbrush, paint in each pentagon with black emulsion or craft paint. Leave the paint to dry completely.

4 Outline the remaining hexagons carefully with the permanent marker pen and the soccer effect will be complete.

5 Install the uplighters according to the manufacturer's instructions, or get a professional electrician to do so for you.

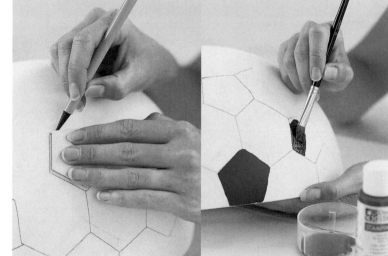

making a soccer pitch floor

easy

2 hours

If the room has a wooden, laminate or lino floor it takes only minutes to create this soccer pitch effect. It's ever so easy to do and it will provide hours of fun and games for any soccer-crazy kid.

tools and materials

- string
- piece of chalk
- scissors
- thick white adhesive tape
- drawing pin
- steel tape measure

1 Using lengths of string as a guide, mark out lines like those on a soccer pitch on the floor in pencil. Since it's important to get the lines straight it may be wise to seek assistance at this stage.

2 To mark out circles and semicircles tie a drawing pin to one end of a length of string and tie the chalk to the other end. Stick the pin in the floor in the centre of where you want your circle, pull the string taut and revolve the chalk around the pin, marking a circle on the floor.

3 When the pitch is marked out satisfactorily, stick lengths of white tape over the chalk lines, beginning with the straight lines. To tape the curved lines, make small cuts in the tape, every 5cm (2in) or so, along the edge of the tape that will form the inside of the curve. As you press it down on to the floor, carefully curve the tape around, smoothing it as you go.

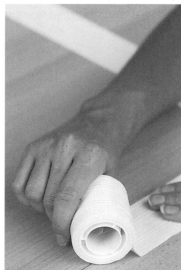

stencilling a roller blind

intermediate

2 hours

Adding a soccer motif to a plain blind is easy and can be done in minutes. This one has been created with a stencil, but you could also use a rubber stamp for a similar effect – or, if you are feeling brave, try it freehand.

tools and materials

- **photocopy of soccer stencil template on page 136**
- **sheet of acetate**
- **craft knife or scalpel**
- **sticky tape**
- **plain roller blind**
- **stencil spray adhesive**
- **old teaspoon and saucer**
- **fabric paint in black**
- **stencil brush**
- **kitchen paper**
- **iron**

1 Make the soccer stencil by photocopying the template to the required size on to acetate. Using a craft knife or scalpel, carefully cut out the stencil. (Alternatively, you could simply tape the sheet of acetate over the top of a correctly sized photocopy and cut the soccer design directly through the acetate, following the picture below.)

2 Spread the roller blind flat on the work surface and then lightly spray the back of the stencil with stencil spray adhesive – don't be heavy-handed with the adhesive, the less the better! Position the stencil on the blind near the bottom edge and press down evenly.

3 Pour a teaspoonful of fabric paint into a saucer and spread out with the back of the spoon. Dip the stencil brush very lightly in the paint and then dab off the excess paint on kitchen paper. When the brush is almost dry start stencilling. Stipple the paint through the stencil; the less paint you use the finer the lines. Carefully peel the stencil from the blind, reposition and repeat across the blind, evenly spacing the motifs.

4 Leave the paint to dry overnight. Heat fix the fabric paint following the manufacturer's instructions.

finishing touches

For this Arsenal fan, it is red and white all the way. Red is one of the most popular team colours but it is also the most difficult to match up. To avoid an eye-straining clash, start with an invariable, such as a treasured team shirt, and then mix paints and dyed fabrics to match.

• To create a focal point, a disused fireplace becomes a goal and the chimney breast is painted vibrant red.

•Recreate the look of a soccer dressing room by fixing smart tongue-and groove-panelling on the walls (see page 92 for instructions) and adding silver coat hooks to a bright red rail to break up a plain wall. These provide the perfect place to display a favourite kit and hanging drawstring bags out of the way.

• Drawstring bags are a real must in kids' rooms as they can be filled with toys and hung up to help keep the room tidy. Use an old pillowcase or cut two rectangles of sturdy fabric and sew them together around three edges with right sides facing, then follow instructions on page 46.

lilac dream

Treat a little girl to a pretty pastel bedroom. Start with a favourite colour – in this case a lovely soft lilac – and take it from there. Choose coordinated gingham fabrics for a soft, pretty look and install tongue-and-groove panelling painted in a darker shade to add contrast and interest and give the room a cosy, country feel.

projects

- tongue-and-groove panelling

- colour-coordinated pinboard

- bedside table

finishing touches

- plant holder shelves

- bedlinen to hide clutter

- pencil-pleat curtains

practical elements

A two-tone wall scheme and stamped border •
add interest to the overall look

Everyday objects can be used for storage •

Tongue-and-groove panelling creates a country feel •

Use a favourite colour to devise an all-round scheme •

Revamp an old noticeboard •

specially
for girls

room to
grow

storage
solutions

1   2   3

tongue-and-groove panelling

intermediate

depends on room size

Give a room a traditional touch with tongue-and-groove panelling. It is not hard to install and requires very few specialist tools. It will, however, need careful measuring – so do not attempt without a spirit level.

1 Acclimatize the unwrapped timber by laying it flat on the floor of the room it is to be used in.

2 Remove all skirting boards and dado rails. Starting in one corner, using a spirit level and pencil, mark out the positions of the battens at dado rail height. Drill holes through the battens into the wall, insert wallplugs and screw the battens securely in place. Repeat, screwing two more rows of battens just above the floor and halfway up.

3 Cut the tongue-and-groove boards to the desired length – the distance from the floor to the top edge of the top row of battening. Starting in the left-hand corner and using a spirit level to make sure it is truly vertical, attach the board by hammering a panel pin through it at both heights of batten (bottom left illustrates panel being pinned to the top batten). Knock the panel pin heads with a nail punch so that they are not proud of the panelling.

4 Continue in this way until you have finished cladding the wall. Finish off the top edge of the panelling with a length of moulding. Attach it to the top of the panelling using wood glue and panel pins. Replace the skirting board along the foot of the panelling. You will need to re-measure the room and cut the skirting board down to the correct size remembering to mitre the corners.

5 Fill all the nail holes with wood filler, leave to dry then sand smooth. Paint the panelling with wood primer and two coats of satinwood paint.

making a pinboard

easy

1 hour

Encourage the kids to keep postcards and memos and at the same time give them somewhere neat to store them. This simple project can be adapted to any style of room and can be completed in less than an hour.

tools and materials

- 70 x 60cm (28 x 24in) rectangle of medium-weight gingham fabric
- 50 x 40cm (20 x 16in) rectangle of softboard or pinboard
- household paintbrush and emulsion paint in white or cream (optional)
- iron
- staple gun
- scissors
- 4.5m (5yd) of 1cm ($^3/_8$in) wide corded ribbon

1 If the fabric is light coloured and the board dark, you may wish to give one side and the edges of the board a coat of pale-coloured emulsion to prevent the board showing through the fabric.

2 Press the fabric and lay it on your work surface face down. Lay the board on top. Fold the excess fabric to the reverse of the board, folding it neatly at the corners, and secure with staples. The fabric should be pulled taut when stapled in place.

3 Cut three 70cm (28in) lengths of ribbon and four 60cm (24in) lengths. Lay four vertical pieces of ribbon side by side on the work surface with a gap of about 9 cm (3in) between each. Lay three horizontal pieces of ribbon over the top of the verticals, again evenly spaced. Lay the covered board on top, face down. Staple the ribbons to the back of the board pulling them taut as you work. When you turn the board to the front you should have a taut grid of ribbon, behind which you can slip tickets, notes and other items.

making a bedside table

Transform a plain wooden crate into a simple bedside table to combine storage and display space while still fitting in well with the country feel of the room. It can be painted in satinwood or emulsion to coordinate.

tools and materials

- steel tape measure
- wooden crate
- handsaw
- **50 x 25mm (2 x 1in) timber**
- medium-grade sandpaper and block
- **piece of 18mm (¹¹⁄₁₆in) MDF,** same size as top of crate
- ruler and pencil
- wood glue
- household paintbrush
- wood primer
- satinwood paint

1 Measure the dimensions of the top of the crate. Halve each measurement and cut four lengths of 50 x 25mm (2 x 1in) timber to give you two battens equal to half the length of the chest and two battens half the width of the chest. Sand any rough edges smooth.

2 Measure the thickness of the sides of the crate; it is likely to be between 1 and 2cm (⅜–¾in). Lay the MDF on the work surface and mark in from each side a border the thickness of the crate. Join up the pencil marks to form a rectangle. Spread one wide side of each of the four battens with wood glue. Position these along the inside lines of the pencil rectangle.

3 When the glue is dry give the crate and its new lid a coat of primer, inside and out, followed by one or two coats of satinwood. As always, allow the paint to dry thoroughly between coats. Sit the lid on top of the crate, the battens should fit neatly inside the crate and prevent the lid from sliding off.

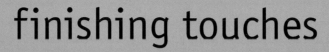

finishing touches

A fun border between the two tones of lilac brings them together and enlivens the look. For speedy results that require no artistic ability, use a ready-made stamp – this cute lamb design is ideal.

• Even everyday objects offer possibilities for storage. Here plant holders have been painted and fixed to the wall to make handy shelves.

• A frilled valance can be used to hide all manner of bedroom clutter. It's a great way of disguising unattractive but useful storage space.

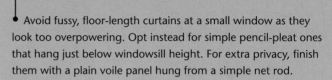

• Avoid fussy, floor-length curtains at a small window as they look too overpowering. Opt instead for simple pencil-pleat ones that hang just below windowsill height. For extra privacy, finish them with a plain voile panel hung from a simple net rod.

space-race room

projects

- rocket cupboard

- space-motif mobile

- a frieze of stencilled space motifs

finishing touches

- silver storage boxes

- striped work unit

- memo board

- countdown panel

Space travel and the great unknown inspire endless fantasies of adventure and excitement, as little boys and girls dream of going on dangerous missions to undiscovered galaxies. With a complete space-age decorating kit and some clever do-it-yourself ideas, you can turn the bedroom of any budding young astronaut into a sci-fi fantasy.

practical elements

Deep blues and space-age silver create a room •
fit for the future that is both fun and practical

A blue laminate floor complements the look and is hardwearing •
enough to withstand the rough and tumble treatment from kids

Good storage is essential in kids' rooms •
so go for a smart metal shelving unit, painted shelves
with funky brackets and bright plastic trolleys
– all perfect for keeping clutter under control

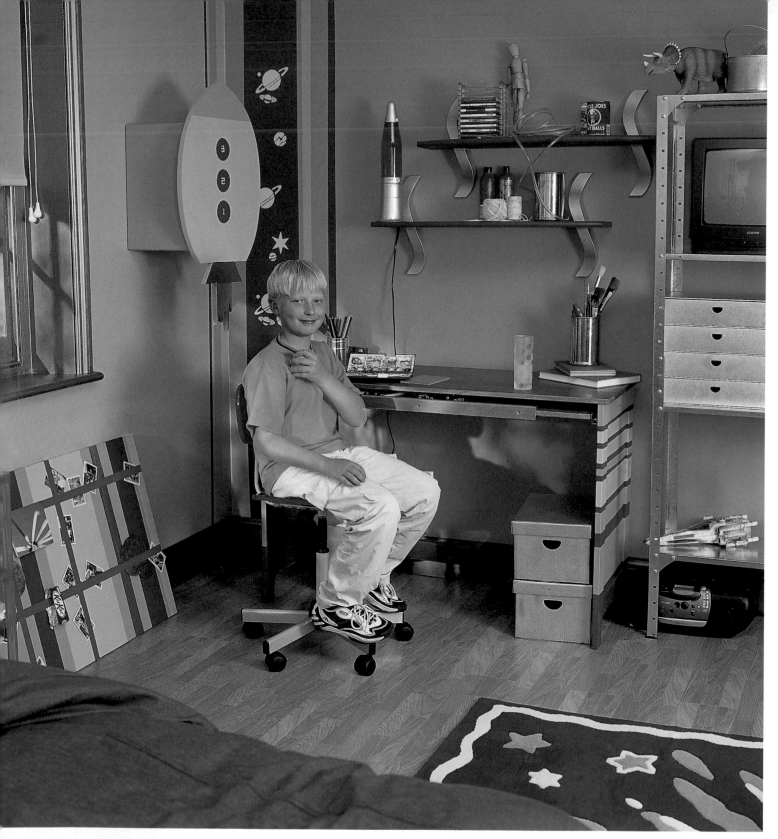

specially
for boys

storage
solutions

study area

room to
grow

play area

97

space-race room

1   2   3

making a rocket cupboard

intermediate

4–5 hours

This rocket cupboard makes a great place to store CDs and computer games. Its basic shape can be the start for whatever otherworld fantasy you like. With help, carpentry-daring kids should be able to complete it themselves.

tools and materials

- pencil
- cardboard
- shallow wooden storage box
- scissors
- piece of 15mm (5/8in) MDF
- dust mask
- jigsaw and MDF blade
- 8mm (5/16in) butt hinges
- magnetic catch
- screws and screwdriver
- household paintbrush
- wood primer
- satinwood paints
- electric drill
- spirit level
- wallplugs

1 Draw the shape of the door for your storage box on cardboard, making sure that it is bigger than the box. Once you are happy with the shape, cut it out using scissors.

2 Place this template on the sheet of MDF and draw around it with a pencil. Wearing a dust mask and using a jigsaw fitted with an MDF blade, cut the door out of the MDF. Fix the door to the box using butt hinges on the left-hand side and attach the magnetic catch to the right-hand side.

3 Prime the cupboard with wood primer and leave to dry thoroughly. Decorate it using satinwood paint in colours to coordinate with the room scheme.

4 To attach the cupboard to the wall, drill holes through the base of the box in each corner. Hold the cupboard against the wall, ensuring it is straight using a spirit level, and mark the position of the holes on the wall with a pencil. Drill holes, insert wallplugs then screw the cupboard in place on the wall.

making a space-motif mobile

intermediate

4–5 hours

Make this simple mobile to hang in a space-themed room for the perfect finishing touch. For a special touch, paint the shapes in luminous paint for a 'glow in the dark' effect.

tools and materials

- scissors or craft knife
- photocopy of space motif templates (see page 137)
- pencil
- thick cardboard
- string
- hacksaw
- bamboo cane
- newspaper
- silver spray paint
- all-purpose glue
- eye hook

1 Cut out the photocopied space motif templates then draw around these on to thick cardboard, drawing four of each shape to produce 12 shapes in all. Carefully cut out the shapes using sharp scissors or a craft knife.

2 Next, cut seven lengths of string approximately 25cm (10in) long. Using a hacksaw, cut a 30cm (12in) length of bamboo cane.

3 Cover your work surface with newspaper and spray the cardboard shapes, string and bamboo cane with silver spray paint, leaving them all to dry thoroughly according to the manufacturer's instructions.

4 Glue a piece of string to the top of one of the cardboard shapes and then sandwich the string using an identical shape. Repeat this with the remaining shapes, then tie the six silver shapes at intervals along the bamboo cane.

5 Attach the final length of string to the centre of the cane, making a loop at the top and securing with a knot. Screw an eye hook into the ceiling and hang up the mobile.

painting a futuristic frieze

easy

2 hours

Give a room a space-age feel with this easy-to-paint frieze. Fluorescent paint works well on a dark background such as this night-sky blue, and will glow in the dark after being exposed to UV light for just a few hours.

1 Using masking tape and a plumb line, mask out vertical stripes of varying thickness on an area of wall. Paint the stripes with dark blue and silver emulsion and leave to dry thoroughly.

2 Photocopy the space motif template provided on page 138. Lay the acetate on top and trace the design in indelible pen. Using a craft knife or scalpel, carefully cut out the stencils.

3 Attach the stencil to the wall using small pieces of masking tape in each corner. Pour a little fluorescent paint into a saucer and dip the stencil brush into the paint, removing any excess on a piece of kitchen paper. Begin to apply the paint to the stencil using a stippling action to prevent the paint seeping underneath the stencil. Once complete, carefully peel the stencil away from the wall and reposition. Continue stencilling in this way until you are happy with the overall effect.

finishing touches

With the cosmos as your theme, there really is no limit to how far you can go: paint a futuristic headboard straight on to the wall, and go mad with silver spray paint and space motifs.

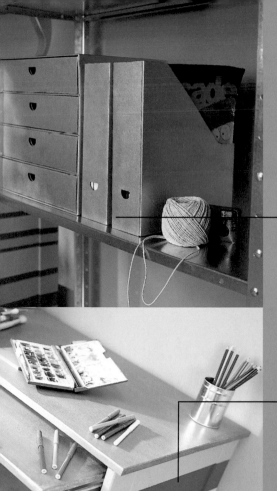

● Help keep things tidy with loads of cardboard storage boxes, ideal for books, and comics – a coat of silver spray paint will totally transform them.

● Jazz up a plain desk with funky stripes to make homework a bit more fun. Just mask off stripes and paint them in different shades of blue. For a really futuristic finish, spray the top with silver spray paint, using lots of thin coats to build up a good finish.

● This fun memo board will also help keep walls free of drawing pins and reusable adhesive. Paint a piece of MDF with stripes of coloured emulsion, attach lengths of ribbon horizontally and vertically and tack them in place on the back of the board – it really is as easy as that!

● Liven up a plain wall with a 1,2,3 countdown panel. Just mask the panel and paint it using emulsion. A numeral stencil completes the look.

hippy chick

To create a wild and wacky teenage den for today's hippy chick, dare to be different and colourful with a bright, hand-painted look that mixes bold stripes and flowers. The trick to mixing patterns with confidence is to stick to the same colours throughout. Here, pale pink forms the perfect backdrop to vivid fuchsia and bold orange. The floral theme is continued throughout using stencils and fabric paints.

projects

- fabric cover for a shelf unit

- beanbag

- funky lampshade

finishing touches

- stencilled ceiling

- bold bedlinen

- wooden floors and soft rugs

practical elements

Durable and easy to maintain, laminate flooring • gives the room a spacious, modern feel

The walls are treated as a blank canvas, giving • teenagers free rein to create their own artwork

The bedroom is turned into a versatile • space, perfect for rest and play

Attractive storage hides clutter out of sight •

1 2 3

making a fabric cover for a shelf unit

intermediate

3 hours

Customize a cheap and cheerful shelf unit with a fitted fabric cover, stamped with a flower design. It can drop down to conceal clutter when there's no time to tidy or pull back to reveal its contents.

tools and materials

- steel tape measure
- wooden shelf unit
- pen and paper
- scissors
- length of canvas or calico (see Steps 1 and 2)
- sewing machine, needle and thread
- dressmaker's pins
- fabric paint in pink
- old saucer
- mini roller
- kitchen paper
- flower stamp (use template on page 139)
- clothes pegs

1 Measure the height, width and depth of the shelf unit. Cut a rectangle of fabric that measures twice the unit's height plus its depth plus 4cm (1½in) for a hem allowance, by the width of the unit plus 4cm (1½in) for a hem allowance. Hem the two short edges of the rectangle of fabric (where the fabric will meet the floor at the front and back of the unit). Mark the centre point of both long edges of the rectangle with a pin.

2 Cut two further rectangles of fabric, 15cm (6in) wide and of a length to match the depth of the shelf unit plus 4cm (1½in). These will form the small side panels to help the cover sit snugly over the unit.

3 Taking one of these smaller pieces of fabric, sew a 2cm (¾in) hem along one long edge. Mark the central point of the other long edge with a pin. Do the same with the other small piece of fabric.

4 Lay the large piece of fabric on your work surface, right side facing up. Place the smaller pieces on top, right sides down, lining up the pins marking the central points. Pin the small pieces to the large piece along the three raw edges of each small piece. Machine stitch a double row of stitching for strength, taking a 2cm (¾in) seam allowance. Trim the seam allowance and cut notches at intervals so that the fabric can lie flat more easily when the cover is turned the right side out. Hem any remaining raw edges.

5 Pour a little fabric paint into a saucer and pick up on the mini roller. Roll off any excess on to kitchen paper. Roll the paint on to the flower stamp. Press the stamp firmly on to the fabric using a rocking motion. Repeat with as many motifs and colours as you want.

6 When the paint is dry fit the fabric cover over the unit. Use clothes pegs to clip the front panel up if needed.

making a beanbag

intermediate

2 hours

Since teenagers invariably prefer lounging on the floor to sitting on chairs, floor cushions and beanbags are always popular items in their bedrooms. This will also look great in faux fur, fleece or denim.

tools and materials

- scissors
- 2m (2¼ yd) cotton lining fabric at least 112cm (44in) wide for the inner bag
- tape measure
- sewing machine, needle and thread
- dressmaker's pins
- 2 bags polystyrene beads – sold in varying weights, ask sales assistant for advice.
- 2m (2¼ yd) fabric at least 112cm (44cm) wide for the outer bag
- iron
- 90cm (35in) zip
- tailor's chalk

1 For the inner bag, cut two 69cm (27in) diameter circles and two 60 x 107cm (24 x 42in) rectangles of cotton lining fabric. Allowing 1.5cm (⁵/₈in) seams and double stitching each seam, join the rectangles along one short side to make a long strip. Join the remaining short sides to form a ring, leaving a 20cm (8in) gap in this seam.

2 Pin and double stitch the edges of the ring and two circles together, right sides facing. Turn right side out through the gap in the side seam.

3 Pour the polystyrene beads into the lining through the gap then double stitch it shut.

4 For the outer bag, cut two circles and one rectangle identical to the inner bag, plus two 32 x 107cm (12½ x 42in) rectangles. Place the two smaller rectangles right sides together and pin along one long edge with a 2cm (³/₄in) seam. Double stitch 8.5cm (3¼in) of seam at each end, leaving a gap in the middle. Press the seam open and stitch the zip in place, double-stitching to make it sturdy.

5 Join the short sides of the zipped rectangle and the larger rectangle to form a ring, as before. Open the zip a little and then pin and double stitch the edges of the ring to the sides of the circles. Turn right way out and insert the filled liner bag.

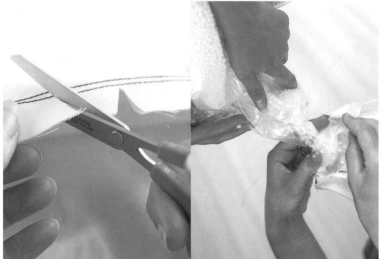

creating a funky lampshade

easy

1 hour

Add a splash of colour to a plain lampshade by attaching short lengths of jazzy cord, ribbon or braid. It only takes minutes but looks fantastic. Work in one colour, or create a rainbow effect with waves of different hues.

tools and materials

- plain lampshade
- bradawl
- scissors
- lengths of coloured wool, fine ribbon or cord in single or contrasting colours
- large darning needle

1 Holding the lampshade firmly, make random holes in it by pushing the bradawl through the shade from front to back, twisting the bradawl to make neat holes. Repeat all over the shade. Don't space them too far apart or the final effect will look sparse and odd.

2 Cut the wool, ribbon or cord into 15cm (6in) lengths, one for each hole, and make a knot in one end of each piece.

3 Thread the large darning needle with one of these knotted lengths and pass the needle through a hole in the lampshade, working from the inside of the shade out. Now make a loose knot in the other end of the wool, ribbon or cord and gently push the knot along its length of wool until it lies next to the shade, before tightening it up.

4 Continue threading lengths of wool, ribbon or cord in contrasting colours until all the holes are filled.

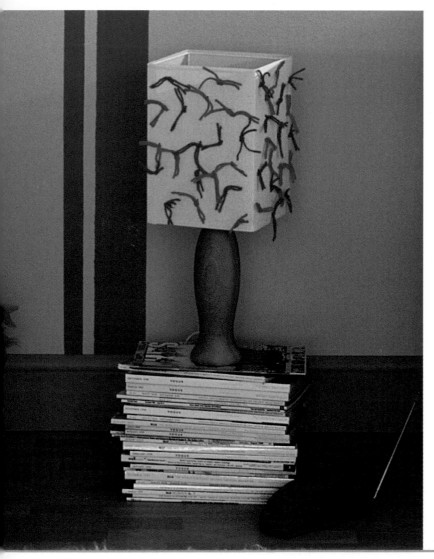

finishing touches

For unique walls, paint on stripes freehand using a roller. For more precise stripes mask up lines with low-tack masking tape and paint them in using a brush. Don't forget to remove the tape as soon as the paint is dry.

● To continue the hand-painted look, decorate the ceiling using stencils to create a casual flower-strewn look (see template on page 139).

● Bedlinen is often bought later to tie in with a room scheme, but this duvet cover, with its happy mix of flowers, hearts and stripes, was the inspiration for the whole room.

● Wooden floors are a practical option for kids' rooms as they are really hardwearing but they can be a bit hard and cold underfoot. Scatter soft, warm rugs to help cosy up the room but always put non-slip pads beneath them to help prevent any accidents.

hippy chick

round the world

Teenagers are notoriously difficult to please, so get them involved in creating a room that reflects their personality and suits their lifestyle. Here, funky retro shades and checked bedding combine in a room to please even the fussiest teenager. If you can't find furniture that complements your colour scheme, you can easily paint your own to exactly the shade you want.

projects

- holey roller blind

- decking memo board

- colourful CD storage

finishing touches

- contrasting shapes and patterns

- revamped old furniture

- instant study area

- round the world clocks

practical elements

A clever painting scheme involves minimal •
work over large surfaces

Pastel colours give a light and airy feel •

A futon bed, which transforms into a sofa, •
is a versatile option for a teenager's room

Unique window treatment matches the airy style of the room •

new york   paris   london

budget

study area

helping
hand

entertaining
area

round the world

1   2   3

transforming a roller blind

Give a plain blind a trendy twist – perfect for the style-conscious teenager! Circles are the easiest shape (make a cardboard template if you can't find a suitable-sized coin) but squares or stars would be effective too.

1 Open out the blind and spread it flat on a large, firm work surface. Weight down the corners with cans or books. Lay the ruler horizontally across the blind, 3cm (1¼in) from the bottom edge. Place the coin on the blind and draw round it neatly with a pencil, drawing a circle every 10–15cm (4–6in) – the spacing between circles depends on the width of the blind.

2 Move the ruler up the blind about 15–20cm (6–8in), check it is horizontal and draw a second row of circles in line with the first. Repeat this process as many times as is necessary up the length of the blind.

3 Carefully cut out each circle using a small pair of scissors and discard the circles of fabric, taking care not to crease the blind.

making a decking memo board

intermediate

4–5 hours

This handy memo board is made from interlinking decking circles and makes a versatile place to pin notes as well as being sculpturally interesting. Any vain teenager will appreciate the addition of a mirror!

1 Sand the pieces of decking to remove any rough areas, then paint each piece in a different colour and allow to dry.

2 Join the decking circles together, as illustrated, using the mending plates with self-tapping screws. Attach a mirror to central decking panel with mirror pads. Screw mirror plates to back of top panel.

3 Fix the memo board on the wall (see also page 52, step 4).

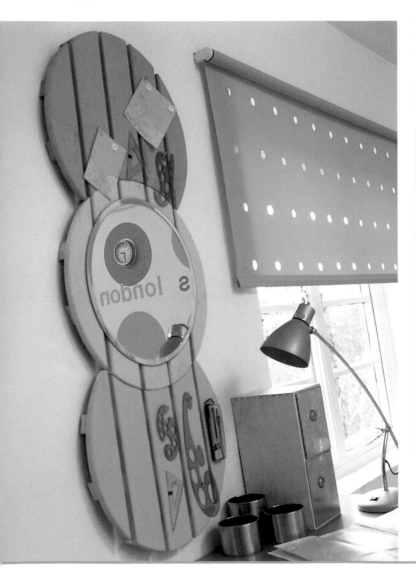

creating colourful CD storage

intermediate

4 hours

This stylish storage unit will give a growing teenager the space required for CDs or other private bits and pieces. It is also a project that they can complete themselves with minimum assistance.

1 Remove the drawers from the chest and give the outside of the unit and each drawer front a coat of primer. When dry repeat with a coat of emulsion – or satinwood for a harder wearing finish. Leave to dry overnight.

2 Measure a drawer front and then cut one of the sheets of tin to these dimensions. Continue by cutting a piece of tin for each drawer front.

3 Choose the letters you want on your drawer fronts and photocopy the chosen templates at the desired size. Cut out the letters then lay the chosen letters on the cardboard, draw round the shapes to make cardboard templates and cut out.

4 Lay a cut piece of tin on a soft surface – a folded tea towel is ideal. Lay a cardboard letter on top of the tin, reversing the letter because you are working on what will be the back of the tin. Using the 'dead' ballpoint, trace around the letter, pressing the nib of the pen gently into the tin. Turn the tin over and review the results. Add extra embossing if required and repeat the technique for the remaining drawers.

5 Secure the tin squares to the drawer fronts by hammering in the upholstery tacks.

finishing touches

Repeated circles and the same three colours help give the room a unified style. Plates and other household objects, even a dustbin lid, could provide the circular templates.

• Checks, plaids and stripes can be mixed together to good effect. Pick three or four colours in similar tones.

• Give a chest of drawers a bright new look with a lick of emulsion paint in shades to tie in with your scheme. First sand the chest to remove the old finish, then paint the panels and drawers in different shades – the choice is yours. Finish with a couple of coats of hardwearing acrylic varnish, leaving it to dry between coats.

• To create an instant desk, paint a length of softwood furniture board with a couple of coats of smooth metallic paint and fix it on top of two three-drawer chests using right-angled mending plates.

• Since the Internet has made communicating with friends abroad quick and easy, why not hang three clocks on the wall to keep track of the time in different countries? Personalize them with the names of cities, drawn on the wall using plastic letter templates and a spirit level, and then carefully painted.

the templates

These templates have been designed so that you can easily enlarge or reduce them in size on an ordinary black and white photocopier. The size depends on the project, the room size and individual preference. These flexible designs can be used to create templates, stencils, stamps and motifs.

121

Making a stencil

- To make a stencil, place a sheet of acetate over the template and use an indelible fine marker pen to trace the design. Lay the acetate on a cutting mat and secure with pieces of masking tape at the corners. Carefully cut out the stencil using a craft knife, cutting just inside the lines. Always take care to cut away from you, pressing gently with the knife and keeping fingers away from the blade.

- Some stencils such as the letter 'O' and 'P' will require 'bridges' to ensure all the pieces remain together. Stencils that require these have white dotted lines on the template, indicating where you should leave a bridge when cutting. (You do not cut out the area within the lines.)

Using a stencil

- Once you have cut out your stencil, spray the back with stencil mount, a special adhesive that will keep it firmly in position while you apply the paint, as well as preventing paint bleeding underneath. Ensure that you spray the adhesive evenly over the entire stencil.

- When you have applied the paint to the stencil, carefully peel it back starting at one corner. Make sure that none of the paint has seeped through on to the back of the stencil, spray with stencil mount and reposition.

- If you have used a stencil with bridges, you may want to hand paint the bridges in once you have removed the stencil. Do this using a fine paintbrush taking care to keep within the edges of the shape.

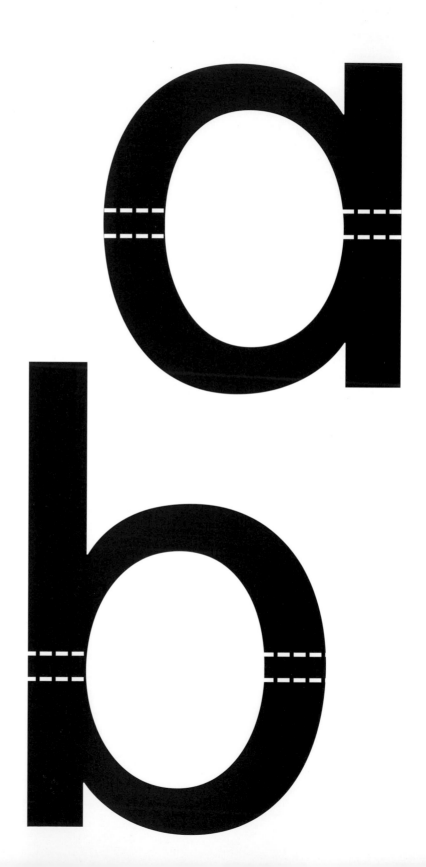

alphabet storage boxes
on cloud nine p.28

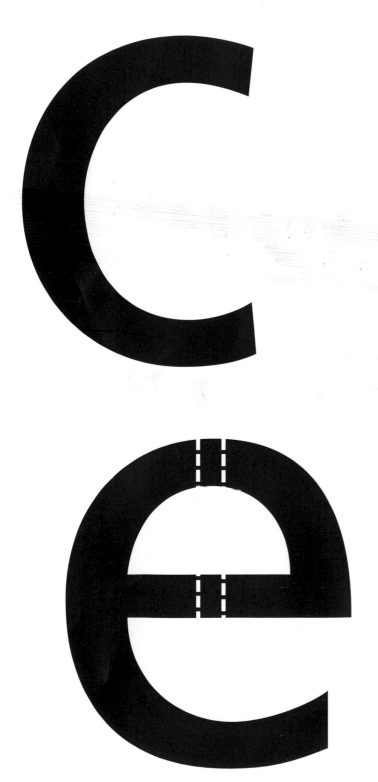

alphabet storage boxes
on cloud nine p.28

f g h

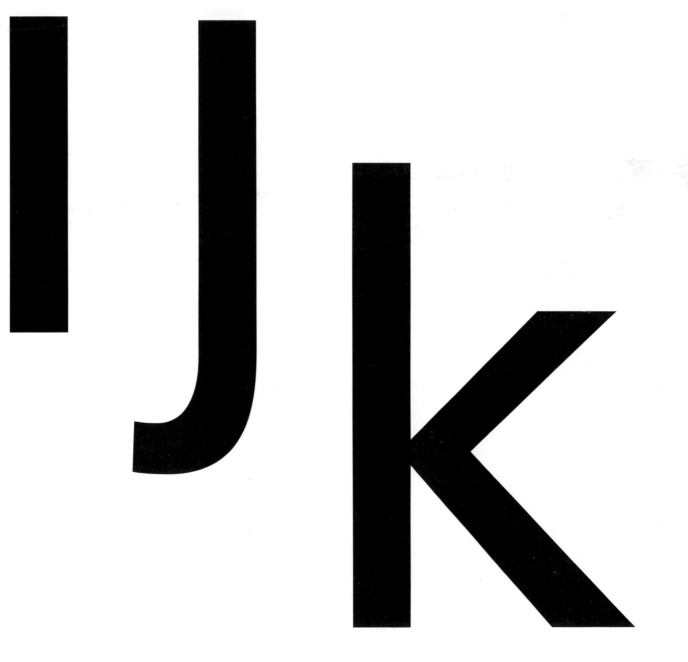

alphabet storage boxes
on cloud nine p.28

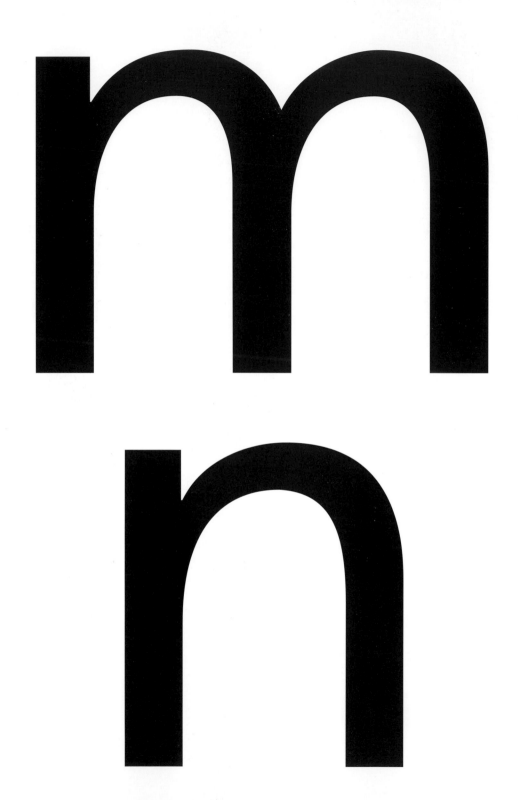

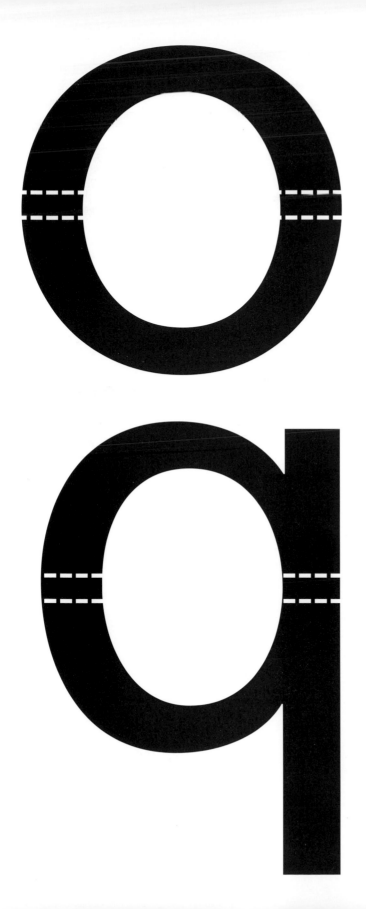
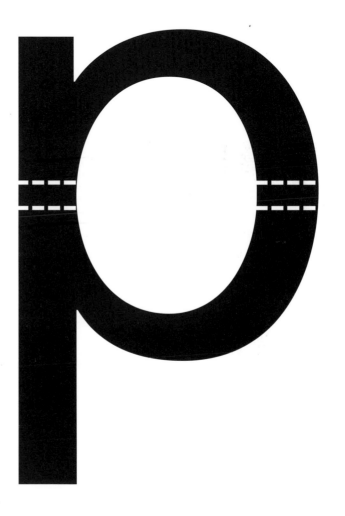

alphabet storage boxes
on cloud nine p.28

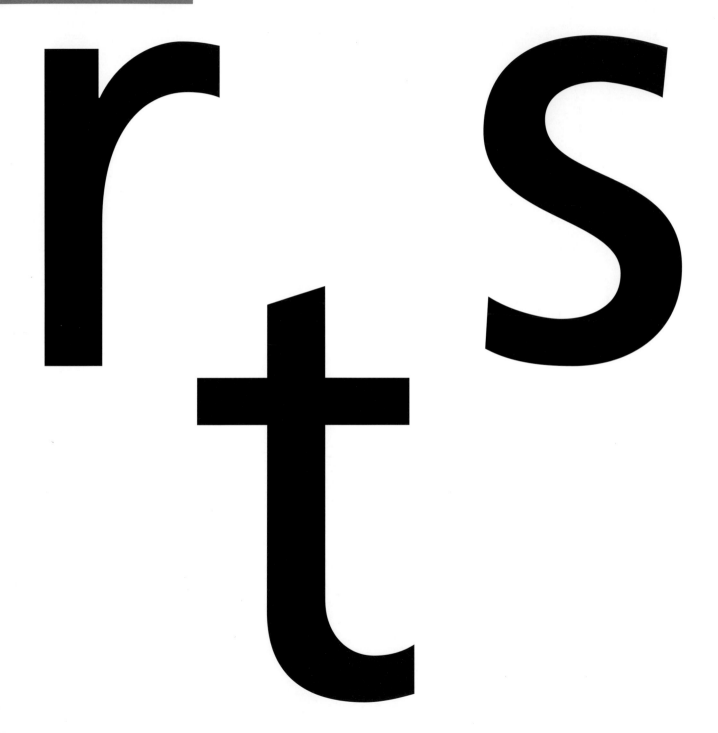

alphabet storage boxes
on cloud nine p.28

alphabet storage boxes
on cloud nine p.28

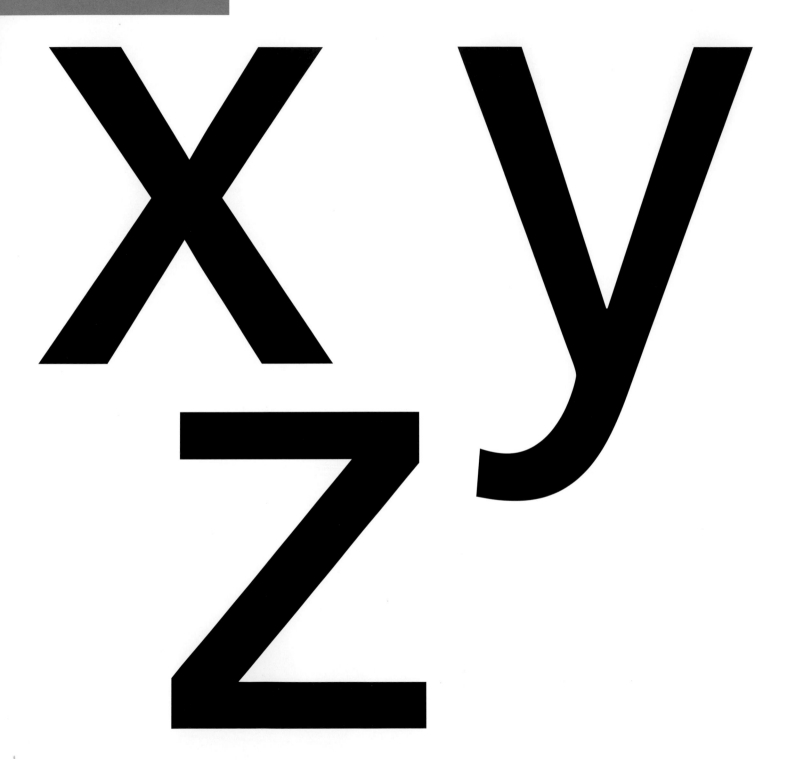

132 the templates

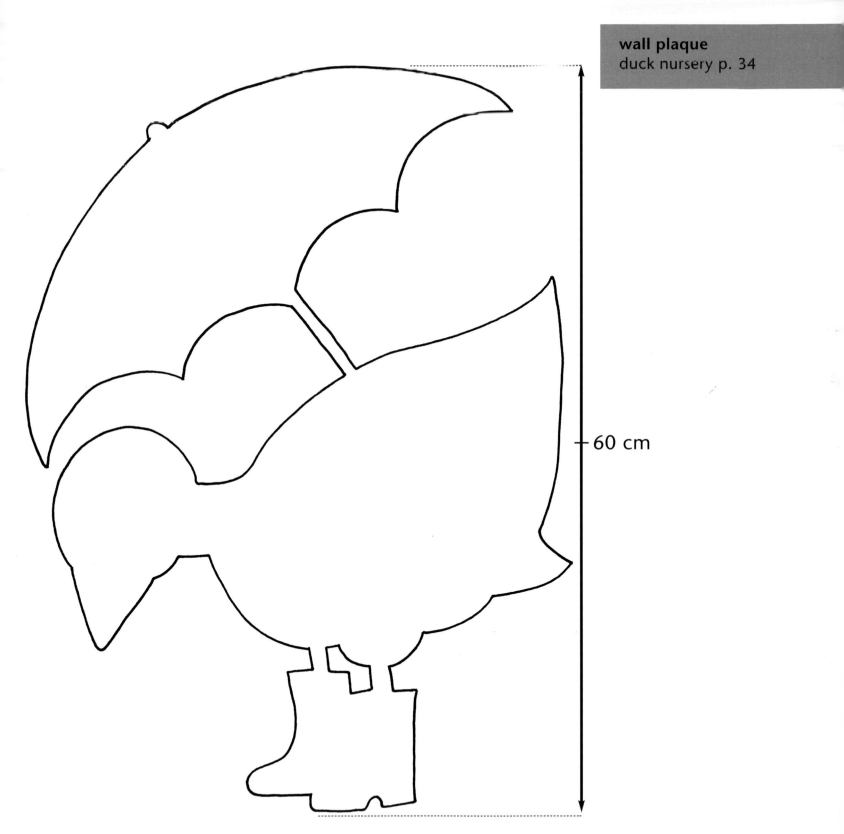

wall plaque
duck nursery p. 34

60 cm

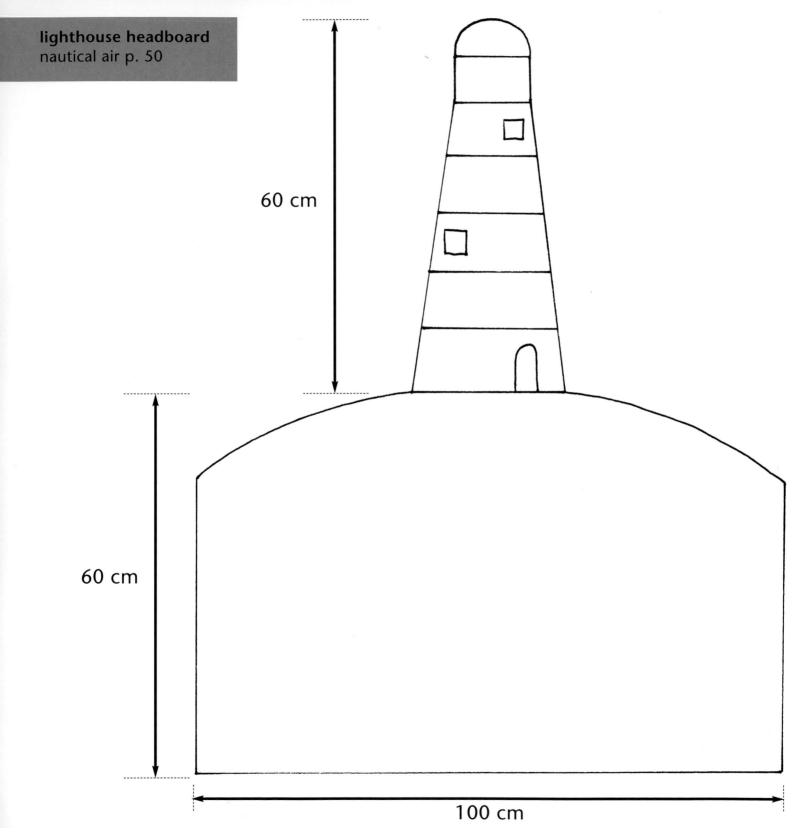

60 cm

60 cm

100 cm

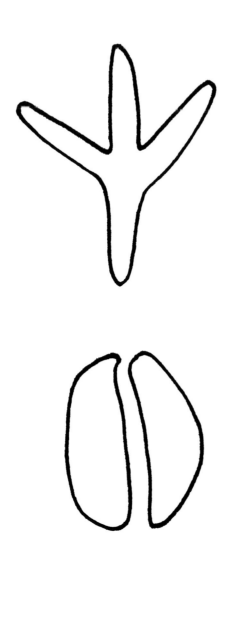

roller blind stencil
soccer mania p. 88

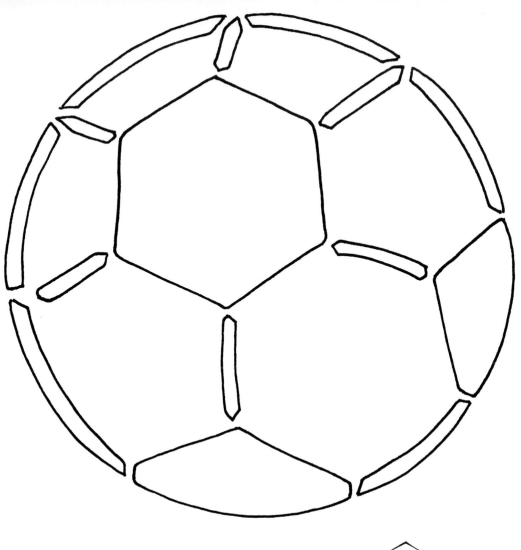

uplighter stencils
soccer mania p. 86

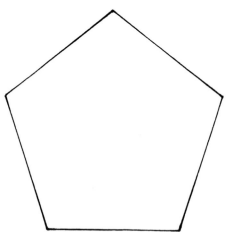

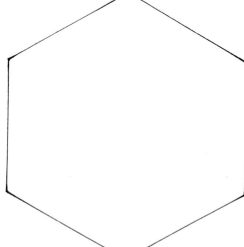

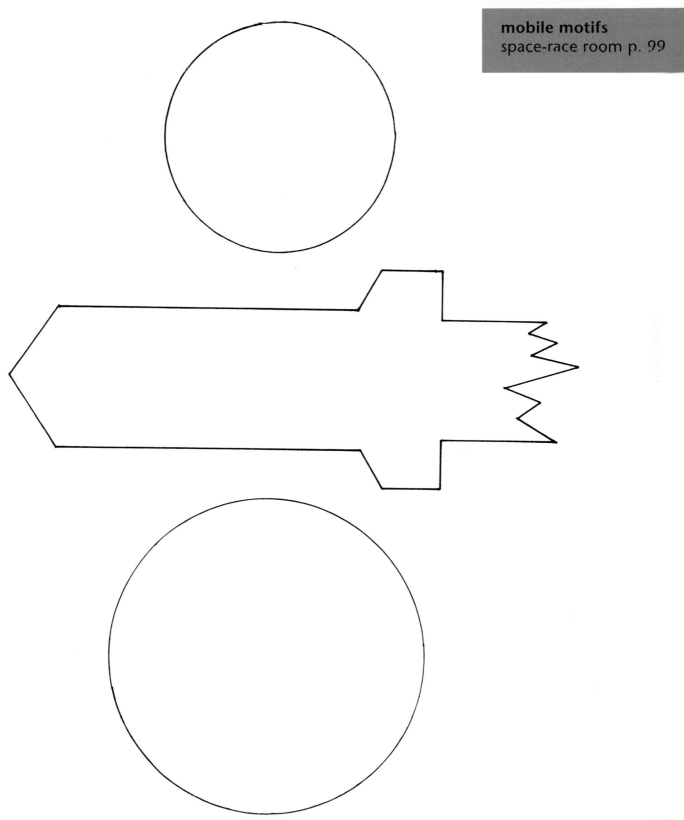

projects index

This index has been compiled to provide an at-a-glance guide to the projects in this book. In some cases the room as a whole is geared towards a specific activity; for example, the Teenage attic room (see pages 114–119) is very much a room for entertaining, and so occasionally a room appears as well as individual projects.

Use this simple guide to find projects specially to suit your child, either by age group, gender, preferred activities, or by your budget or storage problems.

projects for different age groups

projects suitable for babies

projects suitable for toddlers and young children

projects suitable for older children, tweenagers and teenagers

projects for boys and girls

projects specially for girls

projects specially for boys

projects for rooms with limitations

 ## projects on a budget

 ## projects for storage solutions

projects that involve your children

 ## projects kids can help with

 ## projects that will grow with your child

projects for specific activities

 ## projects for play areas

 ## projects for entertaining areas

 ## projects for study areas

index

the authors:

Lauren Floodgate has written about food, DIY and interiors for *Family Circle* and *Home & Ideas* magazines and is currently the Editor of Homebase.co.uk. Author of *The Millennium Party Book*; *The Wedding Planner, The Baby Planner* and co-author of two successful cookery books, she has appeared extensively on television and co-presented a cookery series.

Nikki Haslam has been responsible for producing DIY, style and interiors features at *Essentials* and *Your Home* magazines. Her wealth of design expertise ensures that the pages of Homebase.co.uk are always packed with desirable, fashionable and inspirational roomsets, makeovers and features.

Gill Brewis travelled extensively after leaving college where she studied journalism and has enjoyed a long and successful career in marketing. Gill currently uses her wealth of DIY experience to project-manage features for Homebase.co.uk.

Karen O'Grady has a background in book publishing and has edited a number of illustrated lifestyle titles. Karen is currently the Chief-Sub-Editor at Homebase.co.uk.

acknowledgements:

executive editor Anna Southgate
editor Abi Rowsell
senior designer Joanna Bennett
designer Ruth Hope
icons Ruth Hope
production controller Viv Cracknell
picture researcher Jennifer Veall

authors' acknowledgements:

We would like to thank our hugely talented band of contributors, whose creativity, hard work and expertise helped make this book happen.

Special thanks go to photographers: Simon Whitmore, Lizzie Orme, Lucy Pope and Graeme Ainscogh; stylists: Jane Davies, Nancy Hamilton, Amanda Cochrane, Melanie Coles, Alison Davidson and Petra Boase; and designer and mural artist Bryony Hoad.

Thanks also to the following gorgeous children whose happy smiling faces help bring this book to life: Benjamin Hoad, Joseph Pullen, Florence Cochrane, Matthew Hudson, Ayo & Jumi Akinfenwa, Sid Davidson, Adam Footer, Nicole & Lewis Khan, Rosie Olsen and Emily Sutton. Thanks, too, to the mums and dads.

We would also like to thank Editor Abi Rowsell and Executive Editor Anna Southgate. We have benefited from huge hands on support throughout and they have both been a pleasure to work with.

Thank you all.